3 Weeks
TO AN ORGANIZED HOMESCHOOL

*A Step-by-Step Guide to Organizing Your
Schoolroom, Curriculum, and Record Keeping*

LAURA BERREY

3 Weeks to an Organized Homeschool

Disclaimer: This book in no way purports to offer legal advice on the topic of homeschooling. Please consult other sources for legal information or for help with the homeschooling laws of your state or country.

Scripture quotations in this book are from the King James Version.

3 Weeks to an Organized Homeschool: A Step-by-Step Guide to Organizing Your Schoolroom, Curriculum, and Record Keeping

Short excerpts from this book may be used with appropriate citation.

Copyright © 2016 Laura Berrey

All rights reserved.

ISBN-13: 978-1727043471

DEDICATION

To all the women who have mentored me over the years, many of them without knowing they have done it. To my parents who taught me to love homeschooling. To my husband, who is my hero and constant source of inspiration. To my children, who give me daily delight. And to my Savior most of all, without whom I truly can do nothing.

TABLE OF CONTENTS

1. Why Organize Your Homeschool?... 7
2. How To Use This Book.. 13
3. WEEK ONE: Organizing Your Schoolroom 21
4. WEEK TWO: Organizing Your Curriculum 49
5. WEEK THREE: Organizing Your Record Keeping 73
6. BONUS WEEK: Organizing Your Home And Life 107
7. Homeschooling In Challenging Places 147
8. Conquering Homeschool Clutter 157

Chapter 1

WHY ORGANIZE YOUR HOMESCHOOL?

I love that blissful feeling right after I clean a room. You know what I am talking about.

The bed is made and looks so inviting. The desk is spotless. The wood floor is gleaming. I can sit anywhere in the room and my eye finds . . . nothing out of order.

All is peace. All is calm.

I can rest there, or work, and I won't be distracted by a mess around me.

This is the same serene feeling that relaxes me when I walk into a pleasant hotel room. No clutter. No piles of laundry. No dirty dishes or toy-strewn floors calling my name.

That same serenity is what I felt this year when I organized my homeschool room.

Why Organize Your Homeschool?

All summer we had been on the go. We had crisscrossed the country several times, in several different directions. We had split up as a family, with one or two of us going somewhere and the rest staying home. My husband and I both had heavy speaking engagements. Preparing for that had stolen all of my extra time for months in advance.

At the end of the summer, my husband had flown with our two oldest children to another country for a conference while I stayed home with the youngest four of my children. While he was gone, I was planning to organize for our homeschool year. Instead, that week was punctuated by an unexpected emergency room visit and the backlash of follow-up appointments from that. By the end of the week I was exhausted and had accomplished nothing in the realm of homeschool organization.

My husband arrived back in the country just in time for registration week at the college where he teaches. I was juggling the beginning of the school year for our college with the beginning of our homeschool year and time was slipping through my fingers.

I had this dream, you see, and in my dream our homeschool year started peacefully.

It was my "perfect world" scenario, with excited children and a joyful mother starting the school year in an organized, clean house. All the books were lined up in tidy rows on shelves and all the necessary teaching tools and supplies were conveniently at hand.

All summer I was trying to prepare for this, in the nooks and crannies of my time between other endeavors. All

Why Organize Your Homeschool?

summer I was drawn away from my preparations for this by other more important and more urgent duties.

If only I had three weeks to organize, I could have had my dream start to our homeschool year. But I didn't. Because of the tightness of our schedule this year, I couldn't postpone my homeschool beginning and still finish all our work.

So I just jumped right in.

It's kind of like holding your nose and plummeting feet first into a pool of icy water. I wasn't quite prepared for the breath-stealing impact.

Maybe you have done this before. Maybe you have faced that first day of school with your curriculum still in boxes and a very vague idea of a schedule in your mind.

I knew what I needed to do. I just hadn't had the time to do it.

So I put my kids to work on their studies (we use a DVD curriculum for some classes, so the first few days were rather easy for me), and then I rolled up my sleeves and went to work also.

What I did to organize my homeschool is what I will present here in a simple, day-to-day format.

By the end of the first week, I had a serene, clean, peaceful schoolroom. I used a guest bedroom that was currently empty.

The night I finished my work, I went in and sat down in the schoolroom and relaxed in the utter peacefulness of it. I knew that it wouldn't stay as clean as it was; pencils would soon clutter the desktops, and the room would fill up with bodies and books. But it was organized. I knew where to find everything we needed for school.

My children were so excited to move in and start studying. They enjoyed all being in a room together. The next two weeks flew by with great success as I organized all our curriculum and set up my record keeping.

In retrospect, it was the best way I could have used my time. I now have a system that is easy to use. When a child needs a test, I can put my finger on it in seconds. No more looking through boxes for the answer keys. No more wondering where I should record my grades. Everything is easy to use and easy to find.

This had several strategic benefits for me.

The Benefits of Organizing Our Homeschool

1. I save time.

Yes, it took three weeks to organize my homeschool, but that was an investment in my future. Since I finished that, I have been saving time. Every day precious minutes are redeemed from careless waste because of disorganization. If we get off track for one reason or another, I can just direct the children's attention back to their posted schedules. I know where they should be each day in their studies, and I have a record of what lessons they did each day.

Why Organize Your Homeschool?

2. I save money.

I don't need to purchase another pencil sharpener, three-hole punch, or textbook because we lost our first one and can't find it. I bought almost no school supplies this year because we knew exactly where everything was that we needed. Also, because I saved time by organizing, I am able to prepare healthy meals at home for my family instead of purchasing fast food because I am too exhausted at night to cook.

3. I can enjoy life more.

I can sit and read books to my younger boys. I can build Lincoln Log forts with them, or help them set up their train tracks. My family can sit together and enjoy warm banana bread and homemade breakfasts because I know what needs to be done that day and where each child is in their courses. I am less stressed and more relaxed, which makes for a happier home life for everyone because, as we all know, "If Mama ain't happy, ain't nobody happy!"

4. I save myself from stress.

I can relax in the confidence that we will finish the courses by the end of our planned school year. Even if we skip a day here or there, I know how to make up the work. We have a school year schedule that includes time off for holidays, a family ministry trip to another country, and breaks for various other special events. We have a plan to accomplish all these things in addition to our school work. As we work our plan, we will accomplish what we need to. It is as simple as that.

Do you need to follow my three-week guide in order to

Why Organize Your Homeschool?

experience these same benefits in your own homeschool?

No, definitely not. You may be a naturally born organized person who doesn't even have to think about these things. Perhaps you live a quiet life and are able to devote your summer to planning ahead for your school year. Maybe you do a totally different kind of homeschooling than I do and my ideas just won't work for your family. This is not a one-size-fits-all plan.

On the other hand, I believe that there will be things in this book that will help nearly any homeschooling mother. Something will spark your own creativity or thought processes and hopefully be a blessing. The homeschool forms that I use may not fit your specific situation, but you may find them a great starting point for making your own forms. I hope you will walk away with some new ideas for ways to organize your own family, home, or homeschool.

HOW TO USE THIS BOOK

Congratulations on your desire to increase your efficiency and serenity in homeschooling by organizing!

Just by making the choice to pick up this book and read it, you are already a step ahead of many other homeschooling mothers who are struggling to find joy in homeschooling in spite of a chaotic environment.

What will this book help you to accomplish?

The Take-Away Value of this Book

At the end of this book, if you follow the plan and do the suggested action points, you will have:

- A clean, organized homeschool room or area

How to Use This Book

- An efficient study center for each of your children
- A system for paperwork that confines all papers to a couple of simple locations
- A schedule for your homeschool day
- A lesson plan overview for your whole year
- Lesson plans and assignment sheets for each child for week one
- A complete homeschool notebook for grade keeping and record keeping
- An overwhelming sense of accomplishment and peace

My desire is to help you prepare to homeschool in such a way that your school year will start with a bang. The good kind of bang, not the *dozen-eggs-all-over-the-floor* kind of bang!

My life is crazy busy, and I am sure yours is the same. The weeks fly by as we teach our children by day and participate in other activities at night. If you have the option, don't wait until the first day of school to organize your homeschool. It is much more challenging that way. (But it can be done. I speak from experience.)

As much as possible, I have tried to limit the suggested work for each day to about one hour. Some of this is dirty work, like cleaning. Other times the action points I suggest can be done sitting on the couch while your kids play a board game on the floor in front of you.

Try to involve your children as much as possible in the preparations for your homeschool. Older children can file and label. Younger children can help clean out a closet.

How to Use This Book

If your children are young, you may want to wait until they are in bed to accomplish your tasks. Or, if you are like me, you will prefer to get up an hour early in order to do it before they wake up. Also, feel free to do the suggested tasks out of order. If I suggest shopping for supplies on Tuesday but you run your errands on Monday, switch out the work for those two days.

Don't forget to keep this plan simple. In order to accomplish all I need to do each day, I have to do minimalist homeschooling for maximum education and efficiency. I am constantly and actively looking for ways to minimize the effort involved in homeschooling, and I try to enable my children to help themselves as much as possible. I believe we should give our children increasingly more independence as they get older and watch them take on more and more responsibility for their own schooling! But we must always keep a watchful eye on them to make sure that they are actually doing their work properly and progressing in their education.

Homeschooling and Organizing Simultaneously

Did you discover this book in the middle of your homeschooling year? Are you just beginning your school year but can't sacrifice three weeks of school for preparation?

No problem.

Use this system anyway. You have several options for tweaking this plan to fit your life: speed up or streamline the system, do it simultaneously with your homeschooling, or get help.

1. Speed up the system.

Instead of taking a whole week for each of these tasks, do it in one day. Many of these projects can be streamlined. For instance, you could prepare your homeschool room in one day if you work hard. Brew yourself a cup of strong coffee and speed through your tasks! You can shop for everything needed all at once. You can simplify certain tasks or skip ones you don't need to do.

2. Do it simultaneously with your schooling.

Week one needs to be done in advance, if at all possible. However, I already shared with you how I spliced my first week of the school year together with my homeschool organization. It is not pleasant, but it is possible. Weeks 2-3 can easily be dovetailed with your actual homeschooling year.

3. Get help.

Hire a babysitter to play with your children while you *blitzkrieg* your way through these tasks. Beg Grandma for help. Ask Daddy to take the kids on a date to a play place (or, if you have teenage boys, to a paintball war). Throw something delicious in the crockpot so they walk in the door to some heavenly aromas at the end of the day. If you have older children, solicit their help with the younger ones or with the tasks in order to get it all done. My experience is that children love to help "organize" things. And, of course, they also love the end result of a beautiful school room.

How to Use This Book

Whatever your situation is, do your best and don't stress out over this! God has a plan for your year. You were not gypped if you didn't have a leisurely summer to prepare for your homeschool year. Life may not always seem fair, but God is always good. The tasks on the following pages are not intended to stress you out. They are intended to help you prevent stress by taking charge of your homeschooling in a proactive and strategic way.

Finally, whatever you choose to do, remember that you are a mom with a mission. You homeschool because you love your children and you hope to give them the best possible education in a nurturing environment. Make this homeschool year a fun, joyous time for the whole family!

Before you start

Readers of this book will fall into a couple of different categories. Some will read this book a day at a time and work the plan. Others will read the entire book and afterwards decide which tasks they will work on and when. Yet others will read this book and never do anything. The danger with books like this is that our minds sometimes say, "Hey, I read a book on that topic, so I'm good now." We forget that until we actually *do* something, no change has occurred.

I want to encourage you to do something! So I've got a free gift for you. In the back of this book is a checklist which includes all the action points for each day. But I know that isn't very handy. So I made a download for you with all the action points for all three weeks plus the bonus week. You can print that out and keep it handy while you work. For

How to Use This Book

those who aren't reading the book simultaneously with their homeschool organizing, it will act as a reminder of the tasks you could do each day.

This free workbook is available on the *Resources* page at Homeschoolwithamission.Weebly.com.

May God help you as you begin.

Week One

ORGANIZING YOUR SCHOOLROOM

Chapter 3

WEEK ONE: ORGANIZING YOUR SCHOOLROOM

I grew up in a rural area filled with farms and old houses. I frequently took walks throughout the neighborhood in order to have some quiet time for reflection and prayer. Just up the hill and around the bend from our house was my dream homeschooling house. Not only did the house have horses in the fields beside it, it also had a large sunroom with a huge bank of windows. Every time I passed that house, I thought about how wonderful it would be to homeschool in a room like that sunroom.

Fast forward 25 years.

I have lived in large cities ever since I had children, and have never lived in a house with a sunroom that overlooks fields with horses in it. However, we have had a blast homeschooling; and I have realized that the room itself is

Week One: Organizing Your Schoolroom

not the important thing, but rather the love and joy with which we homeschool.

I have homeschooled in hotel rooms across the States, in other countries on ministry trips, and in tiny bedrooms in tiny houses. I have homeschooled in my bedroom, in my kids' bedrooms, in the living room, and in the dining room at the table. I have homeschooled at my own house and at other people's houses.

I have also travelled widely and seen many other homeschooling moms' schoolrooms. I am always awed by the variety of creative ideas mothers have for their homeschool rooms.

This week we will be working on the physical area where you will be homeschooling. It may not be a large room with a glow-in-the-dark Solar System on the ceiling and Morse code and Latin declensions painted on the walls. It may not have a huge bank of windows to let in light and nature. It probably won't have separate desks lined up side by side. And it doesn't need to.

It can be an extra bedroom, or a converted basement or garage. It may be an attic, or a dining room, or a desk in your child's room. It may be a simple bookshelf in the living room where you keep your teacher's manuals while your children study in various places throughout your home.

Wherever it is, let's make the most of it this week as we prepare for the homeschool year!

Monday

CHOOSE YOUR SCHOOLROOM LOCATION

Where will you homeschool this year? It doesn't have to be the same place as last year. In fact, kids *love* variety. If you need to breathe new life and energy into your homeschool, one of the easiest ways of doing this is by switching up your location. Even if you have a small house, there may be some places you can take over for your homeschool.

Let's consider some options:

A guest room.

How often do you have company? We have company often, including unexpected overnight company. But this is our location for now. As long as I observe my own rule of nightly clean up and I keep the bed made up neatly, we can still have overnight guests at the last minute with a minimum of fuss.

A formal dining room.

Do you normally eat in the kitchen anyway? If you need the dining room only a few times a year, turn it into a homeschool room that can be converted back to a dining room with a minimum of extra work for those special occasions.

Week One: Organizing Your Schoolroom

A finished basement.

This may not be the best option because of the lack of natural sunlight. However, it is a great way to "go to school" in the morning and "go home" in the afternoon.

A finished attic.

This is a little better than the basement option because of the possibility of sunlight. Same pros as the basement.

An extra bedroom.

You don't have one? Would some of your children be willing to share a room in order to make this possible? The biggest challenge may be the difference in the bedtimes of your children. But you can make it work. Having a dedicated schoolroom may be worth the extra effort.

The kitchen table.

The pros? Mom can cook while overseeing school work, and typically the kitchen is the heart of the home. It is fun to all sit around one table and learn not only your own classwork, but other people's also. Family time is maximized with this scenario.

The cons? Having to clean schoolbooks off the table in order to serve lunch and dinner. Books being scattered around in the same location as food. Kitchens and dining rooms require constant cleaning, and working around all those school books is a hassle. However, if this is your only option, do it with gusto! Make a plan for cleaning up before each meal, and have an organized bookshelf where school items are easy to put away.

Week One: Organizing Your Schoolroom

The living room.

Also challenging, especially if you tend to have quite a few unexpected guests show up at your door. However, I have done this with success. You simply must be organized if your homeschool location is in a place that is public. Also, minimize distractions to the best of your ability. Keep the toys in a different location.

Your child's bedroom.

This is one of my least favorite options. We homeschool because we like to be together, not because we want to banish our children to their rooms for eight hours a day! Not to mention, a child's bedroom is the place she will be most distracted. This is where your daughter has whole bookshelves of books. This is where your son plays with his toys. If this is your only choice, plan to remove distractions. But if you have any other option, even if it involves serious sacrifice, jump at it.

Your bedroom.

This is a last resort, in my mind. You need to be able to escape to your room for a nap sometimes. Your room is for romance and rest—not homeschool curriculum, crayons, and random acts of paper chaos. Try to find another option, if you can. Your husband will thank you for it.

Here are some helpful questions to ask when choosing your school room:

1. Can it be closed off?

Can you shut the door on it? There will be times when homeschooling is an untidy endeavor. It is a blessing to

Week One: Organizing Your Schoolroom

have the option of simply shutting the door and shutting the mess out of the line of visibility. It can actually reduce stress in your life. If you can't shut the door, can you curtain it off? Put up a partition?

2. What is the temperature of the room?

If your basement temperature in the winter resembles that of Siberia, you won't want to go there every morning. If your attic is suffocating all year except for midwinter (when it could easily function as a walk-in freezer), you will likewise find it an undesirable location. We homeschool in the one room in our house that is the easiest to keep cool in our tropical temperatures. This makes it a desirable location for my whole family. It is a joy to step into the schoolroom on a hot school day! Make schooling fun by using a location that has a moderate temperature.

3. How big is it?

Can you fit all of your homeschooling supplies and your children in one room? This is a blessing because it frees the rest of the house to be used for the rest of your day.

4. Does it have windows?

Natural light not only eases eye strain, in the long run it can actually make a difference in attitudes and health. Can you open the windows and get fresh air? Don't underestimate the importance of these two things.

5. Does it come with built-in storage or shelving?

This would be a wonderful plus factor. Closets, shelves, and other storage possibilities are necessary for a tidy homeschool room.

6. Does it have an attached bathroom?

How many times has a bathroom break turned into a one-hour playtime because a child became distracted on the way there or back? An excellent schoolroom location has a bathroom nearby.

Monday's Action Points:

- Walk through your house (mentally or physically), and consider each room. Think through the pros and cons of using each space. Especially consider a room you haven't used before. Children love variety! Don't just land on the same space you used last year. Think outside of the box. Decide where you will homeschool this year.
- If you choose to homeschool in multiple locations, is there one place where you can keep all the supplies and books corralled? Things could be taken from there and returned again in order to maintain tidiness throughout the rest of the house.

Tuesday

PLAN YOUR SCHOOLROOM FOR MAXIMUM EFFICIENCY

So, you have picked your homeschool room for this year. Today you will plan it out for maximum efficiency. You will not assemble it yet. Saturday is the day for that. Working smart means thinking things through before executing your plan.

How can you plan your homeschool space for maximum efficiency? You need to start by thinking through your curriculum.

If you use a DVD-based curriculum, you will need special equipment. This is true also if you use an online curriculum. Let's consider first the needs of these two possibilities:

First of all, a DVD-based curriculum requires either a DVD player or a computer. Our family has found that using a computer for school work actually maximizes distractions, not efficiency! So we have chosen to use small personal DVD players for school purposes. These have the benefit of size and portability also; literally, you can take those players in the car with you for schooling on the road, if necessary. You can take them to piano lessons or sports

Week One: Organizing Your Schoolroom

practices. Anyone not involved in the activity could be working on their school. If you have to take the whole family to a medical appointment, they can do schoolwork in the waiting room.

For a great setup, make sure each child has a set of earbuds to use with the DVD player. If two children are taking a class together, you can purchase a splitter which will accommodate two sets of headsets.

On the other hand, online courses require both a computer and excellent internet access. This will take up more space, obviously, than a small personal DVD player. In these cases, you will need a computer and headsets for each child. Consider how you can set up your space to include this type of equipment.

Other types of schooling keep the whole family together as they learn. Unlike the above option, where you can give your children their own desk space, for these kinds of curricula you will want to plan for a large table where the family can all sit together. Ideally, within arm's reach of would be a shelf with each child's school books and necessities. A table is also ideal for homeschooling methods where mom is teaching each child separately in a rotating order.

What else do you need?

Bookshelves are a must. If the desks you are using don't have built-in shelving, try to place a bookshelf nearby. Either put one between the desks (this also gives each child a little bit of elbow room), or set a smaller-sized bookshelf up on top of the desk. You can hang bookshelves

Week One: Organizing Your Schoolroom

on the wall above a desk (make sure it is safe), or you can put a small shelf underneath the desk. Use your creativity.

The room we are currently using, which is also our guest room, comes with a built-in bookshelf that makes it perfect for a schoolroom for four of my six children. Each child has a shelf that is just for them. Above their student shelves I keep teacher's manuals and extra school supplies. At their desk, table, or counter top area, they keep a portable DVD and their pencil case.

If you aren't sure how to make everything fit, try this interior decorating tip: draw a diagram. Measure the room and draw it to scale on paper. Mark windows, doors, closets, etc. Then make paper cut-outs of your furniture to scale and place them on your diagram to see the best possible layout for your school room. This is a great way of trying out different furniture arrangements without making your husband break his back moving book shelves back and forth!

Tuesday's Action Points:

- Consider your curriculum and make a list of everything you will need for your schoolroom. Ideally, schoolbooks and supplies will be close to the study area.
- Small children need shorter-sized furniture. Consider old school desks or student chairs. Can you cut down an old table? Can you use a coffee table?

Week One: Organizing Your Schoolroom

- Do you have the furniture you need? Measure your space. Measure your furniture. Will it fit? If not, what can you substitute? Can you trade out bookshelves from another location in the house? Even a dining room buffet could be repurposed for the school room. An old dresser could become a great storage unit for school supplies. Think outside of the box! If your room has a closet in it, consider building shelves for school books directly into the closet.
- Once you have foraged in your house for furniture to repurpose, if you still have needs, make a shopping list. Plan to check out Craig's list or thrift stores. Rarely will you need to purchase something new. Thursday is shopping day, so plan to check out internet sites before then.
- Don't forget what kind of necessities you need: desk, table, chairs, book shelves, bulletin board, whiteboard, trash can, and a photocopier or printer.
- Spend any extra time you have today moving furniture and any other items out of your homeschool room. Tomorrow we will clean it thoroughly.

Wednesday

THOROUGHLY CLEAN YOUR SCHOOLROOM

Well, it's been fun doing the planning and dreaming. But today we need to roll up our sleeves and do the dirty work of cleaning out the school room.

If you used this room last year, it is entirely possible that the room is still full of last year's school supplies. You have a choice: either take the time now to organize them, or else deposit everything into a box to sort through later. My suggestion is to box it all up and focus for today on the upcoming year.

If you are repurposing a room currently being used as something else, you will also have those former items to move out. For instance, if you will be homeschooling in a guest bedroom, you may need to move the bed and other furniture out of the room in order to clean it thoroughly.

Here is one possible method for cleaning out the room.

Pretend you are moving. Box up everything and transfer it out of the room. If you were moving, would you get rid of some of these items? Would you give them away? Sell them? Throw them out? Maybe you should consider doing that now.

Every single thing should come out of the room. Strip it

Week One: Organizing Your Schoolroom

down to the walls and floor. If you don't have time to go through every item, box it all up in a fairly organized way. Label each box. Stack them in the garage or somewhere out of the way. (Not in your living room!)

Now that the room is empty, clean it. Scrub the ceiling, walls, and floor. If you have carpet, does it need a shampoo? Take a few extra days to finish this task, if you need to. Don't forget to wash the curtains and clean the windows and the light fixtures. You will be surprised how much this will help to lighten and brighten the room.

If there is a closet, empty that also and clean it. Line the shelves with shelf paper, if needed.

Why do I suggest that you remove everything? There are several reasons.

A writer starts with a blank page; an artist starts with an empty canvas. It helps you to rethink a room when it is completely empty. It will be easier to see the best location for a table, a desk, or a new window. (*Just kidding about the window!*) It gives you room to think, to plan, and to consider. For instance, if you will be using your living room, you can plan your furniture placement with all the necessary desks or tables in mind. Perhaps you have to get rid of one of your couches? It is easier to make decisions like this when the room is empty to begin with.

Secondly, it helps you to organize. After all the old stuff is gone, you get to pick and choose the things you add to the room. Add things purposefully, for maximum efficiency. Don't clutter up your beautiful empty space! Make every object count.

Week One: Organizing Your Schoolroom

Thirdly, it helps you to remove distractions. All toys should probably be banned from the school room, so this is a good time to start that process in order to make it as painless as possible. Get your children used to playing with their four thousand Lego pieces in a less distracting location.

Finally, it helps you to make it attractive. You've had those pink drapes in there since Grandma gave them to you? Then now is a good time to take them down and re-think what you really want in there. Perhaps just a valance? Maybe nothing at all, in order to maximize the natural light that comes in through the windows? Pick a new, child-friendly color scheme and redecorate your blank canvas with a whole new beauty! Bright colors, by the way, are energizing, but if you have children with lots of energy already, use calm colors to enable them to focus better.

Wednesday's Action Points:

- ✎ Put a wonderful meal into the crockpot and start up your bread machine. You will be happy you did, later.
- ✎ Gather your cleaning supplies and, if possible, a troop of helpers. Move everything out of the room. (Don't forget to empty the closet.) Collect a batch of boxes and store anything left in the room. Organize the boxes with like items. Label every box! Store in an out-of-the-way location.
- ✎ Take down the curtains and wash them.
- ✎ Unscrew any light fixtures and put them in the sink

Week One: Organizing Your Schoolroom

to soak. Don't electrocute yourself!
- Start with the ceiling and work your way down the walls to the floor. Clean it completely. Try to do it as quickly as possible.
- Put away your cleaning supplies, screw light fixtures back on, and replace your curtains or purchase new ones. Sit in the middle of the floor and sigh in relief as you breathe the luscious scents coming from the direction of the kitchen! Take a break with a cup of coffee or indulge in some ice cream. You did a great job!
- If your children helped with this project, treat them to something special as a thank you.

Thursday

GATHER SUPPLIES

Today we are going shopping. Have you made your list? Do you know the ideal dimensions for each item you need? If you made a diagram of your room, take that shopping with you so you can refresh your mind.

Don't forget to check your budget to see how much you can spend. Don't go into debt for this project.

This also isn't the time to plan a Pinterest brag-fest. Do you know how much damage a group of kids with pencils, pens, and crayons can do to brand new white furniture? And that is before the baby gets into the glue and scissors.

Some places to look for used furniture if your budget is tight:

- Craig's list
- Yard sales
- Thrift stores
- Antique shops
- Bargain rooms in furniture stores or department stores

Honestly, I can't list all the possibilities. Be creative. Ask around. Repurpose furniture you already have. Beg a carpenter—especially if he is your husband or teenager—

Week One: Organizing Your Schoolroom

to make you something!

You don't need a dedicated printer/photocopier if you already have another one. Determine the best location for the equipment you need and keep it there. If you have a home office already set up, it may work best anyway for you to do all your paper work there. But if your printer is located in an inaccessible location, consider moving it to the schoolroom for maximum efficiency.

When planning bookshelves, keep your curriculum in mind. Measure your teacher's manuals. They are too tall for some bookshelves. The DVD cases for our curriculum are even taller than the teacher's manuals, and they only fit on very tall shelves. Also make sure a three-ring binder can stand upright between the shelves.

Remember to plan one shelf space for each child, as well as shelving for each grade level's extra supplies, such as teacher's manuals. So, for instance, if you have four children you are homeschooling, you would need approximately eight shelves. This is approximate, and depends on the curriculum you use and the size of your bookshelf.

When purchasing chairs, consider the movements necessary for each person. Desk chairs with rollers are wonderful for people who move between places frequently. If you have a bad back, take that into consideration when you think about what chair you will need to use. Some chairs will promote slouching. Avoid those if you can. Ideally, your children will each have a chair suited to their height. Small children need child-size

Week One: Organizing Your Schoolroom

furniture.

If purchasing desks, ones with built-in storage are ideal. Drawers, shelves, or a cabinet are all wonderful additions to a desk. Think about the depth and width of the desk if you need to have a computer or DVD player on it as well as textbooks and activity books.

Thursday's Action Points:

- Fix your budget. Stay within it.
- Be creative in where you look. If you don't find everything you need today, make do while you keep on looking. You can still move on with the homework for the future days.
- Be creative in where you shop.
- Take your diagram (or measurements) of the room, just in case you have questions while looking at a piece of furniture.
- Follow your color scheme.

Friday

ASSEMBLE YOUR SCHOOLROOM

You have cleaned and shopped. Now you will reassemble your schoolroom according to the plan you laid out on Tuesday.

Don't forget that we are aiming for maximum efficiency! This means that as much as possible, things will be within arm's reach for the one who needs it. You can be creative about this! Here are some options (we discussed this a little bit on Tuesday when we were planning):

Set a small bookshelf on top of a deep desk.

Place a narrow bookshelf between two desks.

Hang a bookshelf on the wall above the desk. Make sure it is installed in a competent, safe way, or someone could be injured.

Place a short bookshelf on the floor underneath a table or desk.

Be creative in your shelving. Make a bookshelf yourself with bricks and planks of wood. Repurpose other furniture, such as a dining room sideboard, a baker's stand, or old kitchen cabinets. A countertop is ideal for holding larger school supplies like a three-hole punch, a

Week One: Organizing Your Schoolroom

paper cutter, or a printer.

If you have the room, you could plan a floor to ceiling shelving unit. Out-of-use curriculum could be relocated each year to the top shelves, while the lower shelves could be used for current curriculum needs. (There is another way to store off-year curriculum, which I will discuss next week.) If you have tall bookshelves, make sure that they are carefully affixed to the wall. Children love to climb bookshelves. A heavy bookshelf loaded with books could kill a small child. Please keep this in mind.

If all the shelving is inside of a closet, that is okay too. Learn to plan around your circumstances for maximum efficiency. This option might actually help you stay organized, and it has the benefit of a door that can be closed. Here are some tips for closet storage.

Place each child's school books and supplies inside a sturdy plastic crate that they can carry. (Check out thrift stores for these. I have found some awesome ones for only a couple of dollars at thrift stores.) Your children can set their crate beside their desk during school hours and put it away after they are done for the day. The key to managing this kind of system is clearly defining a place for each child's crate inside the closet, preferably on the floor.

Maximize the closet space. Build simple but sturdy shelves up the walls, all the way to the ceiling. If you rent and are not permitted to install a built-in unit, purchase a shelving unit that you can insert into the closet or even use multiple storage or shelving units side by side. If the closet has an existing shelf with wasted space above it, add an extra

Week One: Organizing Your Schoolroom

shelf by using smaller sized bookshelves or free-standing shelf units that will fit above it. Check out cabinet stores for ideas, or look online at closet sites. You can also repurpose. Changing tables have tall, deep shelves. Even a TV cabinet might prove a perfect fit. Work around your limitations.

If you have books and school supplies in a closet and you have little ones who love to get their octopus arms on these things and scatter them like detritus on a seashore, make your life easier: install a slide latch high up out of their reach. Yes, they will climb a chair in their efforts of mass destruction, so make it high.

If you bought new curtains, install them. If you have a white board or bulletin board, hang it! If your room is fairly small and you want to make it visually bigger, use a mirror.

If you have enough space after all your furniture is in place, consider a loveseat placed strategically for reading. It is so much fun to cuddle while working on beginner reading lessons with your kindergartner!

Variety and ability to move around may be key for young boys, especially. If you have several young children, consider placing a fun throw rug or colorful cushions in a corner of the room for reading time. Add a canopy made from lace or tulle for a whimsical tent where smaller children can play while the older ones study. Include a container or two of easy readers.

No toys in this room, if possible! The only exception is a basket of small toys for an infant that you need to

Week One: Organizing Your Schoolroom

entertain while you teach. Toddlers are another story... It is best if they can stay out of the school room or if you can keep them occupied with table tasks or other learning activities while the bigger kids do their school. If your room is big enough, you could set up a small fenced-in area for the toddlers to play. Think through your circumstances for maximum efficiency!

Friday's Action Points:

- Set up your schoolroom for maximum efficiency.
- Think through your storage and shelving options.
- Keep school items within easy reach.
- Try to keep all toys out of the room.
- If you have younger children who are not schooling, plan your schedule and room in a way that enables them to be included or not, as needed.

Saturday

HELP YOUR CHILDREN TO "OWN" THEIR STUDY SPACE

Your schoolroom is completely set up! Hopefully you planned it so each child would have their own space. This is the time to call them into the room and show them where they will be schooling. Let them check the fit of the desk. Make sure they can reach the shelf space you have assigned to them.

Make this a fun time for them. Anticipation for the new school year will explode as they survey their new space. Allow them to choose a picture to hang above their school area or to frame and put on the desk.

Ask for ideas to make the room more fun, beautiful, or organized. You will be surprised by what your children think up! Keep in mind that eye-level for you may not be eye-level for them, so put posters and charts down at their level. What items would dovetail with their curriculum? A timeline? Have them help put it up near their desk. A letter formation chart for a new writer? Have them help you post it on the wall near their study station.

In order to achieve maximum efficiency with minimum input from you, you need to help your children "own" their

Week One: Organizing Your Schoolroom

space. This will encourage them to take the initiative to keep it clean and organized. Yes, you will still need to enforce whatever standards of organization you feel are necessary, but children are more likely to maintain their space when they feel a sense of ownership.

Think about what each child will need. Start making a list of things to collect or purchase. Will each child need his own pencil case or mug for pencils? What about scissors, glue, tape? Do you want one per child? Or will you keep one stash and let them take turns with the supplies? Plan a place for these items.

This is a great way to reveal and to build character in your children. You will notice who is naturally sloppy with their supplies and who is naturally tidy. They need help to overcome these personal character issues!

How about you? Are you a tidy or a messy person? This can be a great opportunity to build your own character while training your children also. It is somewhat hypocritical to require them to clean up their workspace every day if your own space is sloppy.

Saturday's Action Points:

- Give each child their own space.
- Help them to decorate it.
- Provide all the necessary school supplies in a logical location.
- Make a list of anything you still need. We will shop for supplies again next week.

Week One: Organizing Your Schoolroom

Celebration time!

You made it through the first of three weeks and you have accomplished so much! Look around your organized homeschool room and breathe a sigh of relief and anticipation. Next week we will put our skills to work on organizing the curriculum. All those empty shelves will slowly fill up as you dole out school books and plan for the school year.

Two especially challenging homeschool locations that require extra work to set up and keep organized are your master bedroom and your car. If you find yourself homeschooling in one of these locations, chapter 7 will provide extra tips and ideas for how to handle it with grace.

Week Two

ORGANIZING YOUR CURRICULUM

WEEK TWO: ORGANIZING YOUR CURRICULUM

Your homeschool room is glisteningly clean and completely ready for the new school year. Your kids are excited about it and are reveling in the glory of anticipation! But the books are still in boxes, having just arrived from the publisher. Or worse, they are somewhere in storage from the last time you used them. The basic instinct when faced with this situation is to panic and run for the nearest Starbucks.

Don't do it!

This week we are going to get a handle on our curriculum. By the time the week is over, you will have all your children's textbooks and workbooks organized on their shelves and all the teacher's manuals and extras organized for your own use.

Week Two: Organizing Your Curriculum

Everything you need for schooling this year will be at your fingertips, easily located at a moment's notice. Plus, as a bonus, you will have a simple system of long-term curriculum storage set up so that you can easily find all of your other curriculum supplies.

This is curriculum week, so let's get started!

Monday

GATHER ALL YOUR CURRICULUM INTO ONE LOCATION

Today you will collect all of your curriculum. If you have taught these grades or subjects before, you have teacher's manuals and other pieces of your curriculum in storage. Dust off the boxes and excavate what you need.

Is your long-term homeschool storage a mess? Imagine if you could tame your storage once and for all! On Saturday we will tackle this monster-in-the-making. I will share how you can easily get a handle on your other curriculum pieces. For now, just cull what you need for this year and stack all the other homeschool items to one side.

Here is where moms with less of a structured curriculum have a unique challenge: the possibilities are endless! I adore the idea of unstructured schooling, but the blunt truth is that only those who are highly organized can truly succeed at this and turn out well-educated college students who are able to compete in an academic setting. Unfortunately, this kind of homeschooling system tends to attract those who are naturally disorganized, creating a ticking time bomb. Effective homeschoolers realize that they need a system for learning all the details that would otherwise fall through the cracks.

Week Two: Organizing Your Curriculum

If you are unstructured in your schooling and you still have no idea what your children will actually learn this year, let me encourage you to create a plan of attack. This part of your organization will take much longer to complete. Still, it is necessary. Collect all the books, supplies, websites, etc., that you will use this year. And definitely check out your state's or country's laws in order to remain legal.

For those who use a mixed bag of curriculum, decide on the things you will use. Anything within your plan should be placed in your homeschool room or area for organizing tomorrow.

For those using a more traditional approach, this will be much easier for you. If you purchased your curriculum in a boxed set, you have it easiest of all! Just stack your boxes and you are done!

If you have other homeschool supplies lurking in corners around your house, this is the time to collect them and send them back to where they belong. Are your children using their math counting cubes as toy guns? Has your math money ended up in the toy cash register? Did your art supplies wander down to the basement? Were your educational DVDs shelved in your entertainment center?

This is a great game for the children! Arrange a treasure hunt for the buried homeschool jewels. Offer a prize to those who collect the most things from the list. A younger child can scuba dive for missing pieces at the bottom of the toy box. Older kids can scavenger hunt through closets.

This is also a good time to round up the office supplies that you will need for your school year. Markers, crayons, and pencils can be collected from the far corners of the house. Have your children search for rulers, glue sticks, scissors, and anything else that might be needed for school supplies.

Make this fun for your kids. Dole out kisses, hugs, praises, and raisins for your treasure hunters!

While doing this, inquire about where those things ended up. You might find some fun school activities. Have you ever thought of including that toy cash register in your math curriculum? Using Legos as counters for math? They might make great manipulatives for figuring volume and perimeter.

Once you have found all your curriculum and extras, pile everything in or near the homeschool area. Tomorrow we will organize it all!

Monday's Action Points:

- Collect all the pieces for your curriculum this year. Don't forget the things you have in storage!
- Treasure hunt for school and office supplies for your school room.
- Start a list of things you know you need to purchase.

Tuesday

ORGANIZE YOUR CURRICULUM

If you have only one child you are homeschooling this year, your job today will be a cinch! But if you, like many families, are planning to homeschool many children, your job becomes both exponentially harder and more necessary. Let's break this task down into several well-defined steps.

1. Make a pile for each child. Include everything needed for each class. If two children will be taking a class together, make a pile for each class done together.

2. Check that you have everything you need for each course. For instance, make sure you have tests, test answer keys, teacher's manuals, workbooks, and the textbook for each course each child will take. If you see holes in your child's curriculum, put those items on your list of things you need to locate or order.

3. Place each child's student books on their shelf or in their cubbyhole or crate. Keep each course together; for instance, the history textbook should be with the history workbook and any extra student materials. If you have a course where the student has multiple pieces of curriculum, you could corral them all inside a magazine

Week Two: Organizing Your Curriculum

holder or basket for quick organization. For instance, Math classes in the younger grade levels often tend to be bulky with flashcards and manipulatives, so they might need a basket.

4. If you use a curriculum that comes with multiple workbooks, place only the first workbook on their shelf. The rest will go into your temporary storage. We are trying to keep things so simple that even a first grader can keep their student supplies neat and tidy.

5. All the teacher's supplies will go on your bookshelf. Designate one shelf of your bookshelf area per child, and again organize the supplies by course. Keep your tests and test answer keys separate for now. They will go into a different place.

If you accomplished all five of these tasks, your room is starting to take shape. Theoretically, you could sit down tomorrow and start school! However, there are still some things for you to accomplish in order for your year to run smoothly and efficiently. Tomorrow we will go shopping.

Tuesday's Action Points:

- Arrange each child's student materials on a shelf or in a crate.
- Arrange all of your teacher materials in one location, organized first by child and then by subject.
- Separate all tests and test answer keys.

Wednesday

SHOP OR FORAGE FOR SUPPLIES

It is time to go shopping. Here is your shopping list:
- A filing cabinet, drawer, or box with the capability of using hanging file folders.
- Hanging file folders, about 10 per child. Each child should have a different designated color.
- Manila folders.
- Manila envelopes, for test answer keys.
- Three-ring binders, one per child. Preferably in their designated color, or with see-through pockets on the cover. One large binder for you, preferably with see-through pockets on the covers.
- Dividers for each three-ring binder.
- If you have many "extras" for their curriculum (for instance, the BJU Press DVD courses I use come with three-hole-punched parent and student guides), you will also need a binder (or a file folder) for each course.
- Clipboards, one for you. And one per child, preferably in their designated color.
- A pencil holder of some sort for each child. Again, preferably in their designated color.

Week Two: Organizing Your Curriculum

There may be some other possible items to purchase, based on your curriculum. For instance, if you have multiple workbooks for one course, consider investing in a magazine holder for that course. This will corral all the course elements in one place.

If you have a course (such as an elementary math course) with many small pieces or groups of pieces, analyze what you need to use to organize those pieces. Your curriculum may give suggestions for this, such as a shoe box, a tool box, a three-ring binder, a manila envelope, or a plastic bin.

If you need something in which to organize your school supplies, consider purchasing one of the following creative storage possibilities.

An over-the-door shoe hanger with transparent pockets. Each pocket could hold a different item, such as a box of crayons, a stapler, or a whiteboard eraser. With a storage tool like this, you can keep the dangerous items like scissors and the messy items like glue high up out of the reach of little hands.

A tool box or a fly box with a lift-out top level. The little sections on the top level can be used for paper clips, rubber bands, or thumb tacks. The roomier bottom area can house tape, scissors, glue, and rulers.

A small plastic drawer unit. One drawer could hold pencils, another could hold pens, another could hold small containers with tacks, staples, etc.

Each family will have different needs. Analyze your needs and see what kind of storage would best fit that need.

Week Two: Organizing Your Curriculum

There may also be some supplies you need to purchase for your schoolroom, such as a calendar, clock, flag, globe or map, bulletin board, and white board and markers.

If you don't own one already, a sturdy three-hole-punch is a necessity for a homeschool family! Spend the extra money for a high quality one. It will get heavy use.

Wednesday's Action Points:

- Armed with your lists, go shopping.
- While you are running your errands, scout out other organizational tools that could make your life easier.
- Don't give up on something if you don't find it in the expected department. If you are looking in the office or school supply department and don't find what you need, check the hardware department or the bathroom department. I have found awesome desk drawer dividers from the kitchen section: plastic silverware holders or cafeteria-style trays make great pencil, pen, and scissor holders; ice cube trays make great holders for small items like thumbtacks and paperclips. Be creative!
- If you have several children, color code their supplies as much as possible. This makes your life—and theirs—so much more efficient and orderly. (Color coding also works great for toothbrushes, cups, towels, and other items.)

Thursday

ORGANIZE YOUR EXTRAS

It is time to unwrap all your purchases from your shopping trip yesterday. Today we are going to put them to good use.

If you bought three-ring binders, put them on the correct shelves for each child. We will finish getting them set up next week.

Your children would probably enjoy helping you organize all the curriculum miscellany they helped you locate. Each item should have its own storage place and should be kept with the curriculum. If it is an item that will be used later in the year (like the scale you need for lesson 132 in Math), find a place for it in a nearby closet or storage area. If you have no closet, use baskets or bins. Exercise your creativity as you find a place for everything and put everything in its place.

One of the pitfalls of homeschooling, quite honestly, is all the *stuff* that you accumulate after you have done it for a few years. Periodically you need to weed through it all and discard items that are out of date or no longer useful. In addition, you must find ways of organizing the things you choose to keep! Striving for efficiency is a worthy goal. The time you save looking for the stapler can be used to read a book to a toddler. The time wasted looking for the math textbook is better spent making a batch of chocolate chip cookies.

We must redeem time both in our own lives (because the time is short and the work for God is so great) and in the lives of our children. One way of doing this is by keeping our homes and lives organized. On the other hand, we must guard against organization that is ruled by pride or selfishness. If we are stressed out, we won't be "joyful mothers of children." Balance is key.

You should still have a stack of tests and test answer keys. We will deal with those tomorrow when we set up our file box. Today, however, everything else should be filed, boxed up, organized, and labeled for use during the year. This is one reason it is great to have a closet in your homeschool room; you have a place to put all the things you will eventually need.

We already discussed several ideas for storage. Here is my method for dealing with organizational problem areas:

1. Isolate the problem.

One problem I experienced growing up in a large family was the habitual Sunday morning missing shoe mystery. Five minutes before it was time to leave, our entire family would be mobilized on a search and rescue mission for the two-year-old's church shoes. Inevitably one would be found under his bed (or someone else's), and the other would be located behind the couch.

Since we are a ministry family, being on time for church was a priority. I couldn't allow missing shoes to make us late, and I didn't want the stress of searching for them right before we walked out the door. Therefore, one of the first things I did in each house and apartment we lived in was establish a shoe station somewhere near the door. Sometimes it was a basket on the floor of a coat closet. Sometimes it was a hanging shoe rack. The last few years we have used a shoe shelf (like a book shelf but with shorter spaces between shelves). We almost never have to hunt for shoes.

This is a good way to approach any organizational issue: isolate the problem first. Ask yourself some questions. What makes you late? What wastes your time? What causes friction, stress, or irritation in the schedule?

2. Brainstorm ideas.

When my schedule didn't work in the mornings because I was trying to fit too many tasks into too little time, I brainstormed other ways of accomplishing my goals. Can I pass a chore off to a child? Can I accomplish a task later in the day? If breakfast making is what bogs me down, can I lean more heavily on make-ahead breakfasts? This also works for solving storage issues. When you find yourself with a storage or organizational snarl, challenge yourself to think of five creative solutions for that problem. Then you can move on to step three.

3. Give the best idea a try and then continue to adapt.

Week Two: Organizing Your Curriculum

You may find you don't like the result. Move on to your next idea. Don't live with sub-par results. It will continue to wreak havoc and stress in your life. When the piano books weren't working in the storage drawers under our couch, I moved a bookshelf to the side of the piano. When I found piano books and sheet music were still being strewn all over the living room, I bought a few magazine holders to contain the various categories of sheet music. As the number of musicians and musical instruments in our house grew, I realized I needed to make even more adjustments, so I bought each child their own magazine holder for their music. Creative organization adapts to new circumstances.

4. Box it up!

Clutter is a headache. There are people who need the things you are hoarding but don't really use anymore. Box them up and give them away.

If toys move in and out of favor in your house, don't leave them in the middle of the living room floor! Box them up and store them for a couple of months. When they come out of hibernation, the kids will be as gratified as they would be with a new toy.

Box up appliances you don't use. Donate them to a thrift store or other non-profit. Box up items just to get them out of your sight so you can relax in your own home.

This is what we do with the homeschool books and tools that we won't use this year. We box them up.

Week Two: Organizing Your Curriculum

Thursday's Action Points:

- Store all the extras related to your curriculum in the closet or nearby storage area.
- Have your children help with organizing school supplies.
- Give a youngster the job of "pen tester." They can try each pen and marker you find and throw it out if it doesn't work. You might be able to reduce your pen collection to 50% of its original size.
- Each child should have certain school supplies at their own desk: crayons, pencils, pens, etc. Keep extras in a central location such as a tool box or hanging shoe holder with transparent pockets.
- Each child should have a three-ring binder and a small clipboard, preferably in their own designated color.
- Think through your clutter headaches. Isolate the problem, brainstorm ideas, give your solutions a try, and when all else fails, box it up!

Friday

SET UP YOUR FILE BOX

I love my file box.

For several years I've had a problem with my curriculum. All my curriculum was together in one place, and I had to sort through everything else in order to lay my hands on the test my child needed to take. With four children in school, each with approximately eight subjects, I was handing tests out several times a day. Not fun.

So I isolated my problem and brainstormed a solution. Voila! My file box came into being. Now when a child needs a test, I can find it in ten seconds flat.

Here is the method that worked such magic for me:

1. Set up your file box. Insert colored hanging files in each child's designated color, in order of age. You can label them, but if they are color coded, you won't have to.

2. Label manila file folders with the title of each course each child is taking, and place them in the correct hanging folders.

3. File each set of tests in the appropriately labeled manila folder. (For instance, Math 4 tests will go in the folder labeled Math 4.)

Week Two: Organizing Your Curriculum

4. The manila envelopes that you purchased will be used for the test answer keys and they will be placed beside the tests in each folder. So you will have a labeled manila envelope with all your Math 4 test answer keys in the same folder as your Math 4 tests.

I have found that it is easiest to keep the answer keys with the tests. That way, you can grade the test immediately. The envelopes are a practical addition. At the end of the year, the envelope can be placed into a box with the other Math 4 supplies for storage. (Plus this keeps the answer keys slightly more private and harder for a student to accidentally see.)

5. If you have other things to file, they can go into the file box also. For instance, in addition to my student files, I have some extra files which store things like this year's catalogs for my curriculum or ordering forms for next year. Everything I might need for this year is in my file box. Things for other years are not. They have been weeded out and stored elsewhere. This saves me time in searching for the papers I need.

If you don't have a file box, a three-ring binder can be used in the same way. Simply insert labeled dividers indicating the class they are for. A third option is to "file" the test answer keys in a magazine holder. If you put each set of tests and answer keys in a labeled file folder, they will be easy to find. You could also use an accordion file or a wicker basket. The key is to keep them all together in one central location so that they are easy to find and easy to grade.

Week Two: Organizing Your Curriculum

Friday's Action Points:

- Set up your file box. File your tests, test answer keys, and any other papers you need on hand for this school year.
- Anything related to classes not being taught this year should be stacked with all the rest of your curriculum outside of the schoolroom area.

Saturday

ESTABLISH YOUR LONG-TERM STORAGE

Where do you keep all your curriculum materials for last year? The year before? How about your portfolios for all your children? Your records from each year? Do you keep them all in your schoolroom area?

If you have one child that you are teaching, a big schoolroom area, and no other storage possibilities, that might work out well for you.

For all the rest of us homeschooling moms, our mission today is to find an organized way to store our currently unused curriculum materials. What that will include is up to you. You may want portfolios and grades or report cards from past years somewhere you can access them quickly. Or there may be portions of your curriculum that you want close by in case you choose to use them this year. Just choose the items you think you will not need throughout the current year. Let's move them from prime real estate in your school area to an out of the way closet or storage location.

Box it up! My recommendation is that you sort your curriculum by grade level. Therefore, one box will contain only first grade supplies. Another box will hold only second grade supplies. I also recommend that you use plastic storage boxes in order to keep your expensive curriculum materials from being ruined by rodents or moisture. The best way to do this is to purchase stackable plastic bins with lids. Once they are packed, tape them closed with packing tape if necessary. Designate a storage location.

The blessing of this system is that next year you will be able to pull out one plastic bin and you will have everything you need for that grade at your fingertips.

I recommend also that you keep all your records this way. One of the plastic bins could be outfitted with hanging file folders, or you can use your filing cabinet. When the school year is over, transfer the things you need to keep to a folder and file it. This is a simple but effective means of record keeping.

Saturday's Action Points:

- ↪ Designate a location for unused homeschool materials. Box them up by grade levels and store.
- ↪ Store all your files for the past school year in a filing cabinet or a file box.

Week Two: Organizing Your Curriculum

Celebration time!

You have worked hard and made it successfully through week two of your three week plan! Congratulations on sticking with the program.

By now you should have:

- An organized, clean schoolroom.
- Each child's supplies set up for the year.
- All of your teacher's manuals and extras set up for the year.
- School supplies organized for each child.
- A central location where extra school supplies can be easily found.
- A file box for all your tests, test answer keys, and extra files.
- An organized system for storing your unused homeschool materials and records from previous years.

Week Three

ORGANIZING YOUR RECORD KEEPING

WEEK THREE: ORGANIZING YOUR RECORD KEEPING

Wow, your schoolroom area looks great! Your curriculum is already populating the shelves of your homeschool area, and your children have decorated their study areas with personalized artwork or favorite photos. You are in great shape for the new school year.

And yet...

Don't you love the feeling that comes from knowing that all your ducks are lined up in a row? You could start school today, but you might be scrambling when it comes to your record keeping and the rest of your life. (Most of us do have a whole other life outside of homeschooling, but sometimes we have a hard time locating it because of our inefficiency!)

Week Three: Organizing Your Record Keeping

This week you will focus on planning out your school year, organizing your records, setting up binders for your children and yourself, and establishing a system for taking care of all the papers your children are going to start to generate!

By the end of this week you will be truly ready for your school year to begin!

What you will accomplish this week:

- You will assemble your Family Homeschool Notebook, a three-ring binder that will corral your most important papers into one simple location.
- You will make curriculum goals for this year.
- You will prepare a school calendar.
- You will make a daily schedule for each of your children (and maybe everybody else in your house).
- You will overview your curriculum and prepare your lesson plans for your first week of school.

It sounds like a lot of work, but we will take it step-by-step and you will find it is easier to accomplish than you thought it would be.

All the tools you will need for this week can be found at HomeschoolWithAMission.weebly.com.

Monday

ASSEMBLE YOUR HOMESCHOOL NOTEBOOK

Download your free homeschool planner and other resources at HomeschoolWithAMission.weebly.com.

Print out the Homeschool Planner. Included in it are the following:

Homeschool Notebook Cover and *Divider Covers*. Print out as many as you need. Personalize them as you wish.

A *Curriculum and Goals* sheet. You will need one per child.

A *Calendar Sheet* for planning or recording the days you do school.

Several copies of the *Grades Sheet*. You may need one per course per child, but it depends on how many grades you take. If you keep minimal grades for each class, you may be able to print one copy, front and back, for each child. Unlike grade books made for large classes, these are extremely flexible and can be used in many ways. There are two grades sheets in the Homeschool Planner. One has labels for the columns. The other one is completely empty so you can use it however you wish.

Weekly schedule. You will need one per child and one for you. If you have younger children, you may want to make out a schedule for them also. (If your husband has a

Week Three: Organizing Your Record Keeping

challenging schedule you want to keep track of, have him fill one out.)

Weekly Lesson Plan Sheet. One per child per week. You can print front and back to give room for two weeks on each paper.

Weekly Assignment Sheet. You will probably use one per child per week.

Once you have printed these, it is time to assemble your notebook. You can do it in the following order or in any order that makes sense to you:

1. Insert your Homeschool Notebook Binder Cover into the transparent front cover pocket of your three ring binder.

2. Insert several plastic page protectors into your notebook. Slide your personalized divider covers for each child into them.

3. Insert a *Curriculum and Goals Sheet* for each child. (You will fill these out on Tuesday.)

4. Insert your *School Calendar.* (You will fill this out on Wednesday.) If you have no other family notebook or control center where you keep important calendars, such as Little League game schedules or orchestra practice schedules, this is an ideal place for those also. There is a blank monthly calendar in the Planner as well as a 12-sheet labeled calendar for you to choose from. However, you may already have a different calendar or planner you already use. If so, you might want to use this one just for noting school days, holidays, and things like that. If your

children like to know your upcoming family or school schedule, you could also post one of these on a bulletin board.

5. Insert a *Weekly Schedule* for each child. (You will fill this out on Thursday.) You will probably also want to give your children a copy of this once it is completed. I highly recommend you keep a personal copy in case your children lose theirs.

About Your Family Homeschool Binder:

Even if you only use your binder for the pages you have already inserted, you will have a wonderful system for record keeping. All your grades can be immediately entered on the correct *Grade Sheet*. A *School Calendar or an attendance tracker* could be printed for each child for an attendance record.

However, this notebook would also be a great place for keeping important papers. If you typically make a portfolio each year, you could grade the tests and keep them in this binder. Or you can put dividers in this notebook for your children's various classes and keep their tests for each subject here. This would also be a great location for corralling all those special items: the research paper on Shakespeare, the certificate for participating in a music recital, or the journal entries about special field trips. (You can glue pictures of the field trip on the back of their description and slide it into a plastic sheet protector for preservation.)

This notebook will be as useful to you as you make it. I

Week Three: Organizing Your Record Keeping

have found it a wonderful sanity saver.

You can also make a three-ring binder for each child. They probably need something like this for taking notes or keeping activity sheets they are working on. You could personalize one of the divider covers for them for the front see-through pocket of their three-ring binder. The first item in the notebook could be their schedule. If their notebook has both a front and back transparent pocket, you could insert their schedule in the back of their notebook for easy consultation. Otherwise, put it in a plastic sheet protector in the front of their binder. Personalize dividers for their notebooks with the titles of their classes.

I think that you will find this family homeschool binder can revolutionize your record keeping!

One note of caution.

Please research what kind of records your state or country requires. If you reside in the United States, I recommend checking the website of the Home School Legal Defense Association: *HSLDA.org*. This attendance tracker may not fulfill all the requirements of your particular state. For documentation for some of the states with stricter reporting laws, thousands of homeschoolers have found peace of mind using the *Homeschool Daily Log* (learn more about this at Homeschoolwithamission.weebly.org). It was created specifically for homeschoolers living in Pennsylvania—one of the states with the most stringent homeschool laws.

Week Three: Organizing Your Record Keeping

Monday's Action Points:

- Download your free Homeschool Planner. Assemble your Family Homeschool Notebook.
- Assemble your children's three-ring binders.
- If you haven't done so already, research the homeschool laws for your state. Find a way to comply with your state laws; if necessary, purchase the *Homeschool Daily Log*.

Tuesday

MAKING YOUR GOALS FOR THE YEAR

Today we will work on our goals for the year. Goals are incredibly useful if they are SMART goals and if you take time to review them regularly and make plans to fulfill them.

What are SMART goals? They are . . .

Specific

Well-defined, very specific goals enable you to achieve success. For example, a specific goal may be to enroll your child in weekly piano lessons. A non-specific goal would be something like, "Encourage a love of music in my home." With the former, you have a very specific action you plan to do. With the latter, you have a vague idea that is not yet fleshed out.

Another specific goal may be to plan and go on one field trip per month, splitting them up into the fields of history, science, vocational, physical, nature, art, religious, and music. Or you could have the goal of attending three orchestra concerts this year. Or having your child try out for a drama role.

Measurable

You need to know when you achieve your goal. An example of a measurable goal is to teach your daughter to accurately follow one new recipe each week. You can measure your success with a goal like this, because not only is specific, it is measurable. You can literally count the number of new recipes you daughter will know by the end of the year.

Another example of a measurable goal for homeschooling is to homeschool for 180 days before the end of May. Now you have a measurable number you can actually count. Measurability is a key factor for defining success. As the business maxim goes, "You can't manage what you don't measure."

Attainable

Don't aim too low, but also don't aim too high. Your goals should be achievable. For example, don't ask an elementary age child to read *War and Peace*. Don't ask your high school student to read *Pippi Longstocking*. Instead, pick books that are attainable, but hopefully with a tiny stretch so that your child can grow.

If you have as a goal for your child to have the lead role in a homeschool drama, you may have an unattainable goal. Whether or not your child receives the lead role is probably out of your hands. This is why "award" type goals are not usually smart goals. They are not things you can focus on and achieve by yourself. In order to make this a smart goal, you need to focus on something that is truly attainable for your child.

Relevant

Week Three: Organizing Your Record Keeping

Your smart goals should be relevant to your mission in life and to your circumstances. For example, if you live near an ocean, it would be appropriate to teach your children to swim. On the other hand, if you live in Florida or Cambodia, skiing is probably not high on the list.

What goals are relevant to your child's life and to your family's mission? Those are the goals you should single out.

For instance, one of my goals for my child who liked to write music was for her to learn to use a music composition program. It was very relevant to her at that time. If you have a child who loves basketball, a relevant goal would be to enroll him in a basketball league.

Time-oriented

Give yourself a completion date for each goal. For example, you might have the goal to enroll each child in weekly art lessons *during the first semester* and in Latin classes *during the second semester*. Or you might have the goal of completing five lessons from your video course *each week*. You choose your time line, but the choice you make will impact how much you accomplish. Of course, when choosing your time for completion, keep attainability in mind!

You have already printed a *Curriculum and Goals* sheet for each child. List the subject or skill area on the left and jot down some goals on the right. Discuss these goals with your husband; he has insight also on what each child needs.

One of your goals (perhaps the main one) for each subject

Week Three: Organizing Your Record Keeping

would be to finish the curriculum you have chosen for that subject. In order to do that, it will help you to know how many lessons or pages you need to cover each week. On Friday you will overview your curriculum in order to pinpoint this information. I suggest that you write that number down on your goals sheet once you have determined it.

Brainstorm other goals you could have for each subject:

- Field trips to national monuments, battlefields, or museums for their history class.
- A trip to a science museum or the Creation Museum for their science class.
- Biographies of missionaries or important figures in church history for Bible class.
- Reading their Bible daily and memorizing verses or hymns for Bible class.
- Making several easy, child-friendly recipes for math class.
- Learning to shop, keep a budget, and cook for Home Economics class.
- Participating in a piano recital for Music.

In addition to your goals for each subject your child takes, I encourage you to think of skill sets that you want your children to acquire this year and include them on your goals sheet. My husband and I try to take time yearly to discuss goals for our children, including skill sets we wish to nurture in each of our children. What are some of these skill sets? Anything from potty training to learning important computer or vocational skills, depending on the age of the child. Here are some possible ideas:

Week Three: Organizing Your Record Keeping

- Typing
- Using basic computer programs such as Word, Excel, or Power Point
- Using more complicated programs such as Movie Maker, and learning to make and edit movies
- Composing music and learning to use a free music program such as Musescore
- Learning a new instrument or improving on one they already have learned
- Learning record-keeping skills, such as recording mileage or keeping a budget
- Learning Home Economics skills such as sewing, cooking, and meal-planning
- Learning to do home improvements such as brick laying, painting, and carpet installation
- Doing volunteer work for a local non-profit organization or for their church
- Teaching or helping in a Sunday School class or VBS
- Writing a book, learning to blog, or learning to run a small business
- Sports, Scouts, Chess Club, or a Foreign Language
- Learning basic photography and how to use photo manipulation software
- Travel skills, such as booking hotels or airline tickets, navigating airports, or learning to use a subway system

The list is endless. We try to observe where our children's natural interests lie and then tweak them to also make them useful for God's Kingdom. We believe that God made each of our children strategically and uniquely for a specific task for His kingdom. What a shame if our children don't live up to their potential because we didn't take the time while they were young to prepare them!

Many parents assume their children will pick up these skills in high school, college, or the school of hard knocks. Homeschooling parents, however, usually have decided to homeschool because of their burden to train their children for adulthood in a way that schools cannot. We are so blessed! We have twenty-four hours a day to teach and train them. However, much time will be wasted if we have not planned adequately and made goals.

Although we refer to these as goals for your children, they are actually for you. These are goals that *you* will work to accomplish in the life of your child.

Tuesday's Action Points:

- Fill out SMART goals for each of the subject areas your child will study.
- Fill out SMART goals for each of the skill sets you want your child to conquer.
- Ask your child about their interests. Ask them what they want to learn. It might surprise you.
- Get feedback from both your husband and your children about extra-curricular goals for each subject area and skill set.

Wednesday

PREPARE YOUR SCHOOL CALENDAR

There are many ways to plan out your school year. The simplest is to start with the date you would like to begin classes and then establish the date you would like to end. Our school year is often sandwiched between landmarks that won't budge: often a ministry trip bumps right up against the beginning or end of our school year. We have no choice but to finish our school year within those boundaries. If you have no boundaries like that, you have much more time to play with. Decide what you want your school year to look like.

Be creative! Some people like to homeschool for one month, then have a week off. Other families like to homeschool four days a week, with a three-day weekend each week. Some homeschoolers study year round, taking whatever time they want for vacations or trips throughout the year.

Use the *Calendar* sheet you printed to make the rough draft of your calendar. Cross off any dates you know for sure that you need to keep free. Plan as necessary for vacations, holidays, and special events. Then determine what days you will do school in order to complete the legal

Week Three: Organizing Your Record Keeping

number of days (normally 180 days is required). It is good to build in a natural buffer zone for your school year. You never know when someone will get sick and miss a whole week of school. Life happens, and when it does, you want to be flexible. That buffer zone will keep you from becoming discouraged or stressed when unusual events require you to take a day off.

Once you have your calendar worked out, make yourself a monthly school calendar or mark the school days on your wall calendar so that everyone will know the plan in advance. Plan fun events. This is a great way to plan for the goals you made yesterday. Did you make a goal of visiting the Liberty Bell and touring Philadelphia? Plan it into your yearly calendar. Did you decide to visit the Creation Museum as part of your science curriculum? Mark the date on your calendar. Do you hope to take the kids tent-camping and teach them some wilderness survival skills? Plan that for a time of the year with good weather.

Anticipation of special events makes life fun! Your children will tackle their school work with gusto Monday through Thursday when they know Friday will hold a special field trip.

Homeschoolers have a wonderful privilege when it comes to scheduling their school year. You are no longer at the mercy of busy school calendars, so you can shake things up a bit. Vacation in the off-season, when hotel swimming pools are empty and rates are low. Unless you like standing in line for four hours for one ride at Disney World, don't go in the summer. View Mt. Rushmore through whirling snow . . . it's a stunning sight. Go to the

Week Three: Organizing Your Record Keeping

beach when it is cold and your boys won't have to guard their eyes. The off season is a wonderful time to take a family holiday.

Some years we have held classes four days a week, keeping Monday as our family fun day and rest day. It helps to have that time to wake up a little later, do laundry that has piled up, pick up everything that was scattered during a busy weekend, and then have some family time before we start our week.

Even though we cannot do this every year, this is an alternative for homeschoolers that other families don't have. Maybe Daddy has a rotating day off each week? Can you arrange your schedule so your children can enjoy important bonding time with him? If you can't take a whole day off each week, how about a half day?

It is extremely important that you know and follow your state or country guidelines while scheduling your school calendar. Some laws require so many hours in one day in order to count it as a "school day." Other laws require a certain number of days spent studying. Do your research.

Some states require an attendance sheet. This calendar printable could also be used in this way. For those interested in minimalist scheduling: simply mark each day that the child has a school day. Count the days periodically so you know if you are on track. If you are using this calendar sheet as an attendance sheet, print off one per child and keep track of their attendance separately. There will be times when one of them is sick while the others do school. You can mark that day as a "sick" day if your state allows you sick days.

In the Homeschool Planner, I also include a couple of other attendance sheets. One is blank squares, one for each day of a 180 day school year. To use this, you could simply insert the dates you did school. The Attendance Tracker is more of a check sheet. Simply check the box for the days you did school. If you need to report a certain number of hours a day, instead of a check mark, you could put the number of hours.

Wednesday's Action Points:

- Using the *Calendar* sheet, mark your beginning and end dates.
- Mark off any dates you know you cannot have school. Plan the weeks and days you will do school.
- Schedule vacations, field trips, and other fun events. Take advantage of travelling in the off season.

Thursday

MAKE A DAILY SCHEDULE

Scheduling can take on many forms. Some homeschools have rigid schedules, closely resembling that of a traditional school. Some homeschool families live a carefree life, without any schedule at all. Many families, however, opt for something in between. I find my children thrive when they know their boundaries and function within an understood routine. I love the flexibility of living without rules, but I have seen how it can so easily result in nothing being accomplished.

The truth is that habits help us to function efficiently. When you have a habit of waking up at the same time each day, your body will do it almost on auto-pilot! I personally am an early riser. It is rare that I am not up before 5:00 am. My body wakes up, even if my mind tells it not to. This is the power of habit, and it allows me to have quality time with the Lord before the house is busy and noisy! Habit helps me to align my activities with my goals in life.

When you eat food at the same time each day, your body regulates your blood sugar to accommodate that schedule. If you skip a meal or are late, your body goes into a tail spin. Imagine what a completely carefree life could do to

Week Three: Organizing Your Record Keeping

the body of a child! They don't know how to handle an extreme lack of routine.

When you help your children to establish a routine of rising at a certain time, spending time with the Lord, eating their breakfast, doing their chores, and starting school at approximately the same time each day, their bodies automatically adjust to that and it becomes so easy to accomplish everything. If you change the rules on them frequently, you will notice that quarrels are more abundant and they tend to drag their feet.

Today you will make a schedule that will help to maintain routines in your home. Always remember that this is a tool, not a master! There will be days when you will have a very good reason to neglect your schedule. You can do so with confidence, however, that the rest of the week and year will take place according to a plan if you have made (and generally keep to) your daily schedule.

Use the *Weekly Schedule* to map out a school day for your each of your children. Use one per child, and fill in the whole week. There will probably be days that are different from the others because of piano lessons, sports practices, etc. Fill in those special events so that your child knows what is happening each day.

One of my younger children seems to live in a perpetual fog regarding time. He asks if lunch is dinner; he refers to things that will happen tomorrow as if they are a week away; and if we are out all day and come home late, he is the one who asks where we are going next. Children like him especially benefit from a schedule that they can see

Week Three: Organizing Your Record Keeping

and understand.

When you fill out your schedule, you may want to schedule rigidly, down to the half hour. If you do this, please remember to leave yourself buffer zones throughout the day. If you don't, you will find yourself constantly running behind and frustrated about it. With a buffer, you can relax, knowing all will be well in the end.

Some may wish to schedule in a block format. This is a great way to schedule if you want more of a flexible school day. Simply block out the hours you plan to devote to studies, leaving the actual order or length of each class to be decided as you go. (Although the length of classes may change from day to day, it does help children to have a regular order for their classes.)

When children know what is expected as far as school hours, they won't be as likely to request to do other things. For instance, a child who has no schedule may become irritated when asked to do one more class at the end of the day, but the child who can see on their schedule that school goes until 2:00 probably won't ask to play outside at 1:00. If they do, you can simply point at their schedule and say, "Look, honey, school is scheduled to 2:00. After that we can do other things." This takes the onus off your shoulders and places it on the schedule, an impersonal and authoritative object.

If you have a large list of courses to work through, you may find it beneficial to actually schedule classes more like a traditional school does. If you do this, still make sure you leave a buffer zone. We like to finish all homework during

Week Three: Organizing Your Record Keeping

the class, especially for our younger children. This prevents the "uh-oh, I forgot my homework" syndrome. It also allows them to do their homework while the lesson is still fresh in their minds. However, in order to accomplish this, I have to leave a buffer for those days when the homework is heavy. For older children, it may be more beneficial to actually schedule the day more tightly and reserve homework for after school during a homework hour.

You can choose the way you work your schedule, but I do urge you to make some kind of a schedule! If you have many children, you will find the benefits of scheduling are huge! With three or four people vying for piano practice time in my house, we would be in constant turmoil if we had no schedule. With a schedule, we can fit in all the musical practice for piano and other instruments, and I can plan it for a time when it won't wake up the babies who are napping. A homeschooling mama can't ask for more than that.

We each have a sin nature. With two people in a house, there are only two sin natures to work around. But with a large family, the possibilities for strife becomes exponentially larger. We can actually reduce friction and sin in our home by scheduling and thus preventing quarrels.

There are many fine ways of scheduling. If you find you want a more complicated scheduling method than what I offer here, please look up some other ways of scheduling for large families. For instance, Steve and Terri Maxwell's book *Managers of Their Homes* gives excellent ideas for

Week Three: Organizing Your Record Keeping

micro-scheduling a family with many children.

In our family, everyone has a schedule. Daddy lives by a schedule, I have a schedule (mine is more flexible, since I am at the beck and call of others most of the day, but I have that scheduled in), even our preschoolers have their own schedule. Theirs is very "block" oriented and flexible, but they know their routine and it eliminates an amazing amount of whining and crankiness.

What should you do when your schedule doesn't work out? Sometimes the cause is a poorly thought-through schedule. I like to give it about two weeks before adjusting. It leaves time to work out any kinks and discover what things create problems. You will be amazed what shows up: you may have scheduled two children to use the typing program at the same time or to practice piano at the same time. If, however, after two weeks the schedule is not working for some reason, adjust it.

If you find there are certain days when things get behind and you become frustrated, realize that interruptions will happen. Don't allow it to disturb your peace. Instead, remind yourself that that your disappointments may be God's appointments for you. When a boxer sees fists flying at him fast and furiously, he doesn't get frustrated. That's why he is in the ring! He rolls with the punches. Don't be frustrated when you see that a lack of character in you or your children causes glitches in your perfect schedule. Why do you think God gave you children? Why did He give them parents? He is doing a work on all of us. When you find yourself with glitches in your schedule, pray about it. The Lord will show you a way to fix it.

Don't forget to schedule time to achieve your goals for the skill sets you want your children to learn! If you have a goal of teaching them to type, plan time for that each week. If your goal is for them to take a year of piano lessons, schedule in both the lesson and practice time. If you want them to learn to use a computer program, plan to teach them yourself or schedule time for them to go through the tutorials included in the program. The internet is bursting with helpful instructional videos that teach you how to do certain things. Look them up and make a list for your children to watch. (Make sure you have an insanely effective filter if you allow your children access to the internet. This can protect them from temptation and predators.)

Don't forget to schedule some break times! Snacks or play time could be just the thing to refuel your child, break up the day, and give them the mental energy to face their studies again.

Thursday's Action Points:

- Fill out your daily schedule. Don't forget to schedule times of teaching as well as overseeing piano practice, cooking dinner, grocery shopping, running errands, and any other weekly duties.
- Fill out a schedule for each child. This could be a block format or an hour-by-hour format.
- Live by your schedule as much as possible and try not to feel irritated when you can't, for some reason! Be flexible within your routine.
- Pray over your schedule. Allow God to lead you

Week Three: Organizing Your Record Keeping

both in scheduling and in fixing problems and glitches that arise.

Friday

OVERVIEW YOUR CURRICULUM

Your books are all neatly standing in your school area. Today you will consult them one by one and overview them so that you know how to teach each course. This may take some time if you have never taught that particular course before. On the other hand, if you have taught through that book to several previous children, you may already have a good feel for how the course flows.

Your teacher's manuals should tell you how many total lessons are in the book. A core course (like Math), will have one lesson for almost every day of the school year. Other courses may run for only one semester, especially if they are geared for younger children.

Today you need to find out how many days or lessons you need to teach in order to finish that course. Also, it would be good to find out what special equipment or supplies you will need for each course. If you don't yet have those items, you will need to purchase them.

I like to work through this one child at a time. I usually take the time to print off any extra teacher or student materials needed for the course. (This would be a good time to photocopy all the Saxon math tests and timed tests, for

Week Three: Organizing Your Record Keeping

instance!) File any extra material in its logical place: your homeschool binder, your child's binder, or your file box.

You will discover things that surprise you: maybe your younger children can do their heritage studies class for one semester and then move on to science. Or your chosen English curriculum may be light on composition and writing skills. You may wish to supplement with a weekly writing assignment. Maybe your Bible curriculum allows one day off each week for a school "chapel" session. Take advantage of these things. Plan in advance to fill in empty slots or double up on things if a course is particularly heavy.

Many types of curriculum include natural test days. Spelling and math, for instance, might have a test after every five lessons. It helps to know what day of the week you will be testing your child. Plan this into your schedule.

This is a good time to plan out how much of each course needs to be accomplished each quarter of the school year. Grades will be based on that amount of material. You could mark this down on a sheet of paper in each child's section of your notebook or directly on the grading sheet itself.

This is also a good time to go back to your goals page for each child and write down what you want to accomplish under each subject. This helps you to make SMART goals. Instead of making a goal of "finish Saxon math course," you could make a goal like, "finish five lessons and one test each week." Do you see how specific, measurable, and attainable that is? If you accomplish that, week by week, you will finish the course by the end of the school year.

Week Three: Organizing Your Record Keeping

Friday's Action Points:

- Overview your curriculum. Order any special equipment or materials you need for each course.
- Find out how many lessons/pages there are in the course. From that information, plan out how many you need to finish in one week. Write that on your goals sheet.

Saturday

COMPILE YOUR LESSON PLANS

Yesterday we overviewed our curriculum. Today we will fill out the *Lesson Plans* sheet for week one (or, if you are doing this in the middle of the school year, for next week). If you want, you could fill out lesson plans for a month, or for the whole year. I am not that optimistic. No sooner would I fill them out than something would happen to change them, and I would have to recopy everything all over again.

However, taking the information you learned yesterday about how many lessons or pages you need to accomplish in one week in order to finish your course in one year, you will find it easy to do a weekly lesson plan. Just add the next five lessons, for example, or the next five lessons plus one test. Or plan to do ten pages in one week.

This can be as simple as you want it to be. On your lesson plan sheet, simply write the number of the lesson your child will do that day in each subject. On the other hand, if the preparations for that lesson are complicated, you may choose to write down all the extra materials you need or how you will actually teach the lesson. Your choice of curriculum will determine this, but my suggestion is to keep this as simple as possible.

Week Three: Organizing Your Record Keeping

Fill in one lesson plan sheet per child per week, with each course and skill set clearly marked.

When you finish with that, clip your lesson plans to your clipboard (or insert them in your planner). Then, either prepare a *Student Assignment Sheet* for each child or make them a copy of the actual lesson plan you made. Clip these to their clipboards. Definitely do not give your child your only copy! This is your record of what your student did each day. If you have to keep a log of your school work in order to fulfill your state laws, this will help you immensely to fill that out each week.

If you are using a DVD course, you may prefer to give your children a blank assignment sheet and have them fill in what lessons they did that day. (They should already know how many lessons of each course they are to do each day.) Or you can write down what they are to do and have them check it off as they go through their assignments. Either way will work. Check their assignment sheet at the end of the day, as well as any worktext pages or assignments, to make sure they completed all their work.

You may not need to give your child an assignment sheet. If you are a hands-on teacher, teaching each course individually to each student, you could simply keep your lesson plan accessible, note what you need to teach that day, and then check it off yourself.

If your children are very young, they may not be responsible enough to carry through with all their assignments. On the other hand, this is a great tool to teach them responsibility. Instead of them coming to you every

Week Three: Organizing Your Record Keeping

thirty minutes to ask what to do next, just direct their attention to their clipboard. This is fun for them and frees you up to handle more important tasks.

Saturday's Action Points:

- Fill out a lesson plan for each course each child will take for the first week. Keep these in your Homeschool Binder so that you won't lose them.
- Give your child an assignment sheet to check off. Clip it to their clipboard and show them how to use it. Either write the lessons they should do on their assignment sheet or, if they already know to do one lesson a day, have them write down the lessons they accomplished.
- Clip their assignment sheet to their clipboard and prop it up on their study area so that they are ready to start their first week of the homeschool year!

Week Three: Organizing Your Record Keeping

Congratulations!

You have completed all three weeks of your homeschool preparation and organization!

You have put a huge amount of effort into this project and I know you will reap the returns all year. Many homeschool moms wish they could be as organized as you are at this moment.

Because of your diligence and hard work, you now have the following:

- A peaceful schoolroom or area for your children to study
- Well-organized curriculum
- A file box with neatly filed tests and answer keys
- Lesson plans and assignment sheets for next week
- And an easy system for keeping track of attendance and grades.

Week Four

ORGANIZING YOUR HOME AND LIFE

Chapter 6

BONUS WEEK: ORGANIZING YOUR HOME AND LIFE

Sometimes a disorganized homeschool has little to do with the school part and everything to do with the home part. After all, homeschool is a compound word made of two words: home and school. Notice which one comes first? Home, of course. It is the most important word and clarifies what we mean by the following word school.

Without home—in our case—there would be no school. The home is vitally important. In fact, since it is the location where we school, it is truly impossible to separate the two.

If you have a dedicated school room (and actually use it), you have the closest possible differentiation of the two ideas. But even though most mothers have a place that is considered the schoolroom, or a school area where their curriculum is kept and where most of their more formal schooling takes place, the idea of homeschool is that we do it differently! We sprawl. We lounge. We learn by reading, doing, and incorporating all of our senses. We blur lines between home and school, between school and life, and between family fun and learning. And we do it well, because we are homeschoolers!

It's a fun thing.

But it can have its dark side.

Like the fact that the house is never empty so you never get to actually do all your housework uninterrupted.

Instead, you have teenagers sprawled underfoot when you vacuum the living room, you nurse an infant while researching curriculum, and you've learned to swish and swipe the bathroom while potty training your toddler.

Your home, your heart, and your hands are full.

And sometimes all that fullness is hard to organize. I'd love to help you make that a little bit easier.

Many moms already have great systems in place whereby they have truly tamed their home. Even with homeschooling taking up large chunks of their day, they still have a hot meal on the table by six and everybody has clean clothes to wear.

But other moms struggle with these tasks simply because they have never found a system for accomplishing them.

Many times this is because their family grew too fast for them to keep up. Sometimes health issues, either their own or those of another member of the family, have impacted them. Other times they have moved and haven't had time to set their home up for success.

Maybe you can sympathize with these homeschooling moms:

- *"How do you pass the point of feeling like you either keep the house clean or homeschool? I feel like I have to succeed in one area and fail in the other. How can I find balance and get it all done?"*

- *"How do you find time for extra projects? I can manage all my regular chores in a given day, but add one more project to the list and suddenly I'm lost. How do you do it?"*

- *"I can't keep on top of my laundry! I have piles of dirty laundry and piles of clean laundry that needs to be folded. Somehow the laundry never makes it to our closets and drawers. How can I keep up with laundry and cooking and still homeschool?"*

In this fourth week, I want to offer some simple household systems for organizing your home life.

I can't promise you an organized home at the end of this week. We aren't going to be cleaning out closets and picking through our junk drawers. That is not my purpose.

My goal, instead, is to set your feet on the right path by giving you some ideas for systems you can set up this week that will save you hours of time later. I want the few minutes you spend each day this week to repay you every week for the next school year.

Bonus Week: Organizing Your Home and Life

I'm not going to be able to wax eloquent on each item. Like the three weeks you just did, you will read a short explanation of what you should do and then you will have some action points for the day.

My goal is short and sweet. We all know that homeschooling moms don't have a lot of time to spare. I will honor your time.

But I want to give one more word of caution: don't seek perfection. We are going to start systems that are less than perfect. They will get you moving in the right direction. Over time you will find ways to beautify and hone them. But this is not the time to go overboard with a complicated setup. When we set up a meal plan, don't google meal plans and decide you need a cutesy bulletin board with laminated pockets for each day's menu. Later you can research more beautiful, complicated ways of doing each of these systems if you wish to, but not this week! That kind of thing will eat your time. This week your goal is to set up a simple system that you can revise later if you want to.

Simple systems work. Complicated bogs us down. Perfect is the enemy of done.

Let's start.

Monday

FIGURE OUT YOUR "FIVE UNDER FIVE"

I have designated five fast chores that I try to do every single day. They take under five minutes each, but they make a huge impact in my life, in my personal productivity, and in the peacefulness of my home.

Every day I try to do these five chores. When days are really chaotic, I make doubly sure I do them. For instance, right now in my life I have three guests staying in my home and I am also feeding a mission team at least one or two meals a day. I don't have a lot of spare time on my hands. But this just makes it more critical that I complete my Five Under Five.

I can usually do all five chores in under 15 minutes, but at the most they should take no more than 25 minutes altogether. If you can make time in your morning schedule for just 15-30 minutes of quick chores, you can start your day off on the right foot.

What are my Five Under Five?

    1. Make the bed.

    2. Swish and swipe the bathroom.

    3. Throw in a load of laundry.

Bonus Week: Organizing Your Home and Life

4. Prep for dinner.

5. Empty the dishwasher or dish drainer.

Each one of these tasks takes only minutes to do. But the problems that result from not doing them in the morning are staggering. They are small tasks with a monumental impact on my day.

I've figured myself out. I know that if I start with clean, my day will go far better and I will be able to focus on my work. If my home is messy or untidy, I will be distracted and discouraged all day long. This is me. I'm not going to change the way I am, but I can change the environment I live in.

Maybe you aren't like this. Maybe you are able to ignore visual stimuli. I can't. So I work with that.

The Five Under Five list gives me a quick fix for my house and life every single day.

Let's work through them.

Make the Bed

Making your bed is important. Not only does it signal to you that you are up for the day, it will make your bedroom a place of peace. Walking into a bedroom with a sloppy, unmade bed makes me immediately tired and discouraged. But a bedroom with a neatly made bed is inviting and peaceful. This is extremely important to me.

Making your bed also keeps your sheets fresh and clean. There is nothing so refreshing as pulling the covers back on fresh clean sheets at night right before bedtime. If you have children who love to play outside and then come inside and use your bed as a trampoline, you will be glad for the added protection of that blanket or quilt.

Are there times when you can't make your bed? Of course there are. If you have an infant that you nurse and leave to sleep on your bed, don't wake your baby up just to make the bed. Or if your husband works second or third shift and is asleep when you get up, leave the bed (and your hard-workin' man) alone.

Swish and Swipe your Bathroom

We all go in there to get ready in the morning. Whether you are putting on makeup and doing your hair or just brushing your teeth and washing your face, you will likely spend at least a few minutes in the bathroom each day. While I am in there, I swish and swipe.

Sometimes this is not a literal swish of the toilet bowl. Sometimes it is just a quickie cleanup of towels and wet washcloths, emptying off the countertop and wiping it down, and removing any toothpaste blobs from the sink and mirror. Each day I spend just a few minutes putting my bathroom back in order and making it company ready. I save heavier cleaning for another time, but in just minutes I can have a bathroom that I'm not ashamed to let people use.

Laundry

Does it take you just moments to start a load of laundry? If laundry is your nemesis, don't worry. On Wednesday we will nail down your laundry systems so that this chore will only take you a minute. It takes me less than five minutes to start a load of laundry, but that is because I have a working system. Even if you don't have a working system, start today with a quick load of laundry. If grabbing a full load of dirty clothes from scattered locations all over the house will be too much work, instead just grab a load of towels or dirty sheets. Toss it into the washing machine and start it. There. Done. You have just automated your life.

Dinner Prep

Dinner prep can take a long time. When I list this as one of my five under five, I'm not saying you can make your whole meal in that short amount of time. What I mean is to have a plan and do your initial legwork. In other words, in five minutes you can have a menu plan worked out in your head or on paper (we will talk about this more tomorrow), defrost the meat, make sure you have all the ingredients, and maybe even start part of your meal. Keep it under five minutes and move onto the next item.

Empty the dishwasher or dish drainer

Having an empty dish drainer (I don't own a dishwasher) is paramount to keeping my kitchen clean. If the drainer is empty, dirty dishes can be immediately washed and set in it to dry. But if I have to empty the dish drainer before I can wash dishes, it is likely that at nine o clock tonight, those dishes will still be sitting, dirty, in my sink. I can't have that. So I try to spend just a few minutes emptying clean dishes from the drainer.

This is even more important if you have a dishwasher. Go open it and look inside. Are the dishes inside it clean or dirty? If clean, put them away immediately. It should take you less than five minutes. If they are dirty, go ahead and fill it up and run it. Dishwashers are supposed to simplify our lives, but for some women they are counterproductive. Let it be a blessing to you! Empty it every morning during your five under five time.

These five chores under five minutes each have made a huge difference in my life. Regardless of what my day holds, or what kind of craziness is going on in my home, or who is currently living with us, I know the "Five Under Five" will start my day out right and keep me pointed in the right direction. It's a simple, speedy approach to getting your home under control each morning.

Monday's Action Points:

- Do you have a memorized short list of the most important tasks for keeping your home running smoothly? If not, take a few minutes to sit down with a cup of coffee or tea. Ask yourself what the most important tasks are, and how you can accomplish them early and simply. The easier and simpler those tasks are, the more likely you will be to do them every morning.
- Why don't you try this tomorrow morning? Allot yourself 25 minutes to quickly accomplish these five fast chores. See how long they take you. Time yourself, and try to beat the five minute deadline for each. Afterwards, ask yourself what you could have done to streamline the process. Could you do all five tasks in 15 minutes? Ten? What would it take?

- Maybe "Five Under Five" isn't enough for your household. Maybe your front door opens into a lobby or living room and you want that to be included in your morning regime so that when unexpected guests show up, everything in their direct line of sight is tidy and neat. Go for it! Figure out a way to make it happen in just a few minutes. You don't need to limit your list to five. The number doesn't matter. Just keep them fast and simple to accomplish.
- Whatever your tasks are, and however many you have, write them down right now on a three by five card. Keep it on your refrigerator or clipped to your calendar until you have done them so many times you can do them in your sleep. The worst possible thing would be for you to wake up tomorrow unsure of what these tasks are. If you have to try hard to remember them, you probably won't do them at all.
- Make sure these tasks are numbered in the general order in which you should do them. Try to make it a logical order. If you brush your teeth as soon as you wake up, swish and swipe might be the first chore on your card.
- Ask a friend or family member to hold you accountable for the first ten days of doing this list. If you can do them every day for ten days, you will be well on your way to creating a habit!

Bonus Week: Organizing Your Home and Life

SIMPLIFY WITH MEAL PLANNING

If there is one thing you can do to make your home run more smoothly, it would probably be meal planning.

What is so amazing about meal planning?

Let me share some of the benefits of meal planning.

- You will eat healthier food
- You will shop more efficiently
- You will eat more variety
- You will save more money
- You will save time
- You will save yourself stress
- You will be able to use up food you have before it goes bad
- You will be able to prep in advance

But the question is, what is a quick and simple way to meal plan?

In the *Homeschool Planner* you downloaded there is a weekly meal planner sheet. There are probably thousands of freebies like this online. However, you don't need a printable. A 3 by 5 card will do. Or a whiteboard. Or a chalkboard.

I've used various things throughout my life, but the most common thing I am using right now is simply a 3 x 5 card with my menu plan listed on it. Simple and easy, but very effective!

I'm one of those people who likes to live on the pantry principle: you buy what food is on sale or the foods you use regularly and then you create meals around what you already have. I try to keep a variety of meats, beans, sauces, and broths (canned or frozen) on hand with which to cook. Our family eats a lot of meals made from scratch, so that means my basic staples are necessities. They are the building blocks for my meals.

You can do your meal planning many different ways. I try to keep it simple with a macro-plan. Our macro-plan for meals is to eat the same basic foods for breakfast, switching between 3 or 4 menu options. Our noon meal is often our biggest meal, and I try to make that more heavy on the meat and veggies. We almost always have some form of fresh fruit. Then our night meal is usually either leftovers, soup, pasta, or sandwiches. I don't plan all of the side dishes or fruits and veggies in advance. I typically just buy them and serve something at every meal.

Once a week, I list out the major meals for that week and see what I need to buy in order to serve those. I put those items on my shopping list. Then, each day I pick a meal from my weekly master list that will fit that day's agenda best. Sometimes these days are planned in advance, if I know a certain meal needs to be served on a certain day. This is especially true when I have guests.

But on the other days, I just pick off my master list. I do this early in the morning so that there is time for cooking.

Bonus Week: Organizing Your Home and Life

During various times in my life, I have used more complicated systems of grocery shopping and meal planning. Your meal planning will probably evolve also, as your family changes. This is what is working for me right now.

I would like to suggest that you use the simplest method possible for now. My goal is to get you up and running with organized systems for your homemaking. I'm not trying to make your life more complicated.

If you don't know where to start with this, here are a few quick and easy suggestions for easy menu planning.

If it's Friday, it's pizza.

With this kind of meal plan, you have a general category for each day. The actual recipe may change from week to week, but you maintain your outline. Monday could be pasta, Tuesday could be fish, Wednesday could be soup. You pick your categories and each week do a recipe from that category.

Family favorites

I like this for a starter meal plan. Ask your children and husband what their favorite foods are and plan them out for the next 2-3 weeks. Just jot them down on a card and make a grocery list for the ingredients.

Subscription Plan

Do you want someone else to pick the recipes for you and make your list? Purchase an online subscription or try the book *Saving Dinner* by Leanne Ely. The meals are healthy and easy to fix and she includes a shopping list for each

Bonus Week: Organizing Your Home and Life

week's menu plans.

There are many other ways to plan your menu. I have a whole chapter on ways to practice creative meal planning in the book *Life Management for the Busy Homeschooling Mother*. But you don't need to find the perfect way right now. After all, perfect is the enemy of done. Instead, just pick a way to meal plan and make your menu for this week. Base your shopping list on it, after you have checked your freezer and pantry to see what needs to be used up.

Tuesday's Action Points:

- Pick a method of meal planning and make a list of meals for the rest of this week.
- Make a list for next week.
- Want to make your year easier? Make a four-week list and rotate it every month.
- Take it a step further and create one four-week list for each season of the year.

Wednesday

LAUNCH YOUR CAMPAIGN AGAINST DIRTY LAUNDRY

Clothes should come with a disclaimer like, "absolutely necessary but requiring a lot of work."

When it comes to providing clean clothes for our family, there are several steps we need to master. First we need to collect dirty laundry, preferably in one place and not scattered all over the house and the bedrooms. Then we need to transport that laundry to a place to be washed. For most of us this will be our own laundry area in our home, but some mothers may need to go to a laundromat. Thirdly, we need to prepare our clothes to be washed. Then we need to wash and dry them. After this, we must either fold or hang them. If necessary, clothes need to be ironed. Finally, they need to be transported and put away.

Problems with laundry arise when we get bogged down in one of these steps. Some moms never get started because there is no system in the house for collecting dirty laundry. Everybody does what is right in their own eyes, which means that dirty clothes collect in the bathroom, under beds, and on the floors of closets.

The first step in creating a system for laundry is to

Bonus Week: Organizing Your Home and Life

determine the location where dirty laundry needs to go. You will need to inform your family of this; and if it is a new location, you may need to spend a couple of weeks reminding people where you expect their dirty laundry to be.

I believe in centralizing as many things as possible in my home, so I have one place where all dirty laundry, without exception, is put. Right outside my bathroom door is a big wicker laundry basket with a lid. Our normal lifestyle includes baths for every family member at night, so this is the logical location for my family. Your family may be different. It doesn't matter where your dirty laundry gets collected. What matters is that you have a clearly defined place for it. You might want this to be in a laundry basket in each person's room, or you may want it to be in a central location.

My suggestion is that you base this solely on who is responsible for washing the clothes. If your children wash their own clothes, you will want them to have their own laundry baskets. If you or one other person is responsible for all of the laundry, however, I highly recommend that you make life easy on yourself by collecting all dirty laundry in one central location.

You don't need to think too hard about this step. Just take a second to designate a location.

୨୦ My dirty laundry location:

The second step is to transport the laundry to the washing area. In order to set up a system, you need to designate who will do this and when. This is a wonderful chore for a younger child. I like to start my laundry early, so I vacillate between making this a chore for a child or reclaiming this task. However, *who* does this doesn't matter, as long as somebody does it and they know exactly when and how often to do it.

- Who will collect the dirty laundry:

- When will it be collected:

- How often will it be collected:

Our third step in creating a laundry system is to determine how laundry is prepared for washing. Some moms bypass the sorting step by having a laundry basket with three compartments: one for lights, one for mediums, and one for darks. The benefit of this is that a smaller family won't need to wash all their loads in one day, so they can slowly collect a full load and wash it as necessary.

This doesn't work for my family. We do laundry every day, so my method of transporting laundry is to carry all my laundry down to my laundry area every day. Typically this is three loads: one of towels and wet washcloths, one of darks, and one of lights. But I don't sort it until it is downstairs near my washer. I sort one load immediately into my washing machine, and sort other loads into empty laundry baskets nearby. As a homeschooling mom, my mornings are busy, so I choose the load that is easiest to fold as my first load of the day. Typically this is either a load of jeans or a load of towels and washcloths.

Bonus Week: Organizing Your Home and Life

As I put laundry into my washing machine, I turn clothes right side out (especially those pesky jeans), and pretreat anything that needs it. If something needs to be soaked, do it right away. Keep a basin near your washer and pretreat as you go.

    ❧ How I sort laundry:

    ❧ How I prepare laundry for the washing machine:

    ❧ How I pretreat laundry:

The next step is simply to wash and dry the laundry. If you have a machine for each of these jobs, that is wonderful! Do you thank God for that? There are many people in this world who have to wash all of their laundry by hand. Your job is immensely easier if you have a machine.

Still, you need to determine how often you will wash your clothes, and how you will do it. I wash laundry every day, and I have certain points throughout my day when I reboot my laundry by transferring one load to the dryer and adding the next load to the washer. I typically start the first load early in the morning, reboot at breakfast, reboot in the middle of the morning during snack time, reboot again at lunch, and do whatever still remains late in the afternoon before dinner.

If you only have one load or two to do every day, it is much easier. Put a load of laundry in at night before bed. In the morning, as soon as you wake up, transfer it to the dryer and if necessary, start the next load. Your first load should be done by the time breakfast is over and your next load should be done by lunch.

    ❧ When I start my first load:

    ❧ Reboot Times:

When your clean clothes come out of the dryer (or off the line), you have two choices: fold or hang. There is no "third bird." Throwing all your clean laundry into a basket and setting it down somewhere in your home is self-defeating. It will be a wrinkled mess before you get to it. Do yourself and your family a favor and either fold your laundry right into a basket (or several, depending on your system) or hang it immediately.

My M.O. is to fold all my laundry directly from my dryer into one clothes basket. I don't sort at this point. I just fold. (You are welcome to sort while you do this.) Any item that would be hung in a closet gets hung immediately on hangers on a pole by my dryer. This one step of hanging right away can save me hours of ironing time.

Where do I get my hangers? Thank you for asking. All of our empty hangers go into the dirty clothes basket that is kept right outside my bathroom upstairs. I carry them down with my laundry. This saves me quite a bit of time. It also prevents me from running up and down the stairs every time I find a hanger. I just toss them in the basket for the next day. Simple works.

    ❧ How I fold my laundry:

Bonus Week: Organizing Your Home and Life

❧ How I hang my laundry:

Ironing is a necessary evil for many people. You might live a lifestyle that precludes most ironing. Using your dryer properly and hanging clothes immediately can heavily reduce your time spent ironing. But there will still be some items each week that need to be pressed. I encourage you to plan a time when you will do all of your ironing for the week.

❧ When I will iron:

Transporting your laundry and putting it away is the last step. I hope this isn't the one that bogs you down! By this point, you are almost done. If you let this last task slip, too often all that clean laundry ends up all over the house and needs to be re-washed before it can be worn. My goal is to save myself that extra work.

I encourage you to make it your goal to have all the laundry put away once each day. This may be at night before bed, or it may be in the morning before starting school. But please designate a time when, as often as possible, this chore is finished completely.

I've mentioned that I fold my laundry directly from my dryer into a basket. This means that I have to add an extra step later: sorting. As laundry gets finished, I carry the baskets of folded clothes to my bedroom. There I take a few minutes to sort everything out on my bed into stacks for each person. Then I call my children to grab their pile and put away their clothes. I put away my husband's clothes and my own. Sometimes I have my younger children help me by being my messenger boys and carrying clean clothes to the correct person's bed.

- When I will sort and transport laundry:

- Who will put it away:

If you have faithfully filled in each blank throughout this chapter, you now have a system for your laundry. Please don't get bogged down by perfection. Simple works. Begin your system today. If you lack the appropriate equipment, like laundry baskets or a place to collect dirty laundry, put it on your list for the next time you go to the store. But you don't need fancy equipment! The most important thing you need is a system.

Wednesday's Action Points:

- Fill in the blanks.
- Inform your family of any changes.
- Teach your children to properly put away their laundry in their drawers and closets.
- Train your family in daily putting dirty laundry where it belongs.
- Purchase any needed equipment.

Thursday

MAINTAIN HEALTHY HABITS

One day in church one of my foreign friends came and sat down next to me. "I really wanted to thank you for your talk about hobbits," she said.

I panicked for a moment. When had I talked about hobbits? Surely, never! I've read *The Lord of the Rings*—who hasn't? But I had never given a talk about it.

She kept on speaking while I tried to rack my brain for a reasonable explanation.

And then I heard her words, "I've been trying to do some of the things you suggested and I've made a list of hobbits to do every day."

My smile grew genuine as I realized that her accent had thrown me. Habits. She was talking about the Bible study I had shared on habits.

Phew!

I don't know if hobbits are healthy or not—after all, they eat two breakfasts—but you as a homeschooling mama sure can be! I want to encourage you to pick some healthy habits to accomplish every single day, and to jumpstart your brainstorming, I'm going to share mine:

- 4 By 4
- 5 a Day
- V8
- Learn and Burn
- Screen and Caffeine Curfews

I don't do all of these every single day. I wish I did. I try to. But I do them as many days as I can. I consider them to all be daily habits, even if I occasionally fail to accomplish them. They are each important to my health and to my energy level.

Here's the thing: as homeschooling moms, we are with our children all day. Have you ever noticed how much energy they have? If we aren't bolstering our energy levels with healthy habits, they are going to leave us languishing in the dust. It is a little ironic that we, who need the energy the most, have the hardest time fitting a healthy lifestyle into our busy days. We have to focus on the most important things in order to move the needle on our own health goals.

Let me encourage you to join me in doing these five streamlined healthy habits.

4 by 4

Water is the most important part of a healthy diet. Most women do not get nearly enough water on a daily basis. Do you?

Did you know that 60% of your body is made up of water? Your body needs water to function well. In fact, headaches, tiredness, and hunger can all be signs pointing to a lack of water.

I decided several months ago that I was going to start drinking a gallon of water a day on most days. Some days I just can't. But I live in a hot zone and sweat a lot, so I knew I was probably dehydrated. I also felt lethargic and tended to drink too much coffee, an *unhealthy* habit of mine that frequently caused late afternoon headaches to sprout. So I knew I needed to make this change.

Was it easy? No.

Drinking water wasn't hard. But keeping track of how much I drank, making sure I had water nearby all day, and spending more time than normal in the bathroom was a challenge. I tried several different methods, but finally settled on one that really worked for me.

Here's what I did.

I decided that if I drank three liters of water, the water I drank at my meals would definitely equal another liter, so that would put me at four liters. I finally realized that if I filled three one-liter bottles of water each morning and tried to drink one before breakfast, one before lunch, and one before dinner, that would give me my gallon of water for the day. I didn't want to be waking up all night long, so I put a cap on my drinking at about 4:00. By 4:00 pm, I was supposed to have drunk the last of the three one-liter bottles. When I added in my mealtime water, I would be very close to drinking four liters of water by 4:00 pm.

It worked! Taking the big goal of a gallon a day and splitting it up like that made it easy for me to check in on myself. Sometimes I would find myself chugging the end of my liter a few minutes before sitting down to my meal.

That's great, because drinking water 30 minutes before your meal actually helps stave off the hunger pangs and encourages you to eat less. I needed that, because I was also trying to lose weight. It was a win-win situation.

My 4 by 4 rule, in addition to (presumably) helping me to lose weight, also helped with my regularly recurring headaches and prevented me from drinking as much coffee or other drinks. With the exception of special occasions, I entirely cut soda from my diet. And I cut back on other drinks like iced tea. All of this aided me in my health and fitness goals.

But the best result was that I felt better and more energized all day. A hydrated mama is a happy mama!

Are you getting enough water each day? Is it adequate to keep you hydrated and energized? If not, try this 4 by 4 life hack. I assure you, it will help you to feel better.

If you can't stand water plain, add some ice and lemon slices. I have a one-liter mason jar that I love drinking from. It is the perfect size and shape for lemon or cucumber diffused water, and it looks so pretty and refreshing that it makes you long to drink from it!

5 a Day

It really shouldn't be five a day, health experts tell us, but 8-10 servings of fruit and vegetables a day. Lest that sounds like far too much fresh stuff, let me remind you that a half cup of veggies or a medium size fruit is considered a serving. But to make it easy, let's think of it as a half cup.

Both fruits and vegetables are better raw and fresh, so if you eat one serving of fruits or veggies with every meal and two extra snacks a day of raw crunchies, you just completed your five a day.

Buy the fresh foods you like, if you are just starting out with this. Neither potatoes nor corn can count. But a fruit shake? That totally counts, my friend. So start with one of those. If you throw lots of ice cubes in it, you are also boosting your water! In hot weather, this is a luscious treat.

In colder weather, we tend to eat more cooked veggies, especially in soups and stews. However, all year long you can add bananas, raisins, or frozen berries to your cereal. Add lettuce, tomato, and onion to your sandwich. I love a big green salad, but if you don't enjoy your fruits and veggies plain, you can always add them to something for that extra nutrition!

V8

I'm a busy homeschooling mom. I don't just forget to drink my water; I also forget to take my vitamins. So I have a motto for that too. V8. Vitamins at or before 8:00 am and 8:00 pm. I don't take many vitamins, but I have a few that I should spread out throughout my day, and this schedule does the trick. Do you ever forget whether you took your vitamins? I sure do! My brain is usually on something else while I pop my pills. A daily pill keeper can solve this problem. It is the perfect tool for making sure you don't overdose. If the pill is there, you didn't take it. If it isn't, you did. What an awesome crutch for a forgetful mom!

Learn and Burn

There are two ways to do this. The first way is for you to continue homeschooling your children while you are making your dinner. Put the meat in the pot to cook and then teach one child their math lesson while you give a spelling test to another. They are learning while you—or rather, your dinner dishes—are burning.

This the is the kind of "learn and burn" I *don't* recommend doing.

Instead, I highly suggest you do the healthy learn and burn. This includes listening to a podcast, sermon, or an audio book while you are walking, jogging, or doing whatever exercise you do. I currently do this in the morning before breakfast. As part of my normal morning routine, I spend about 30 minutes outside in the fresh air, learning new things while burning off some calories. It's a great way to start your day.

Screen and Caffeine Curfews

Sleep is super important. We don't get enough of it. As a nation, we are wired and tired. Part of the problem, sleep expert Shawn Stevenson says, is that we are not observing simple curfews.

I do best when I curfew my caffeine early in the day, like by early afternoon, and have no—or little—screen time after dinner. If you struggle with getting enough sleep, these two types of curfews can make a big difference.

Healthy habits are important for maintaining your energy and staving off sickness.

I'm afraid that many moms—especially homeschooling moms—fail to take the time needed to prepare for and do these healthy habits, and I think I know why. As busy homeschooling moms, we are so caught up in constantly meeting the needs of other people that we often put our own health on the back burner. We might even feel like we are being selfish if we take the time to exercise, for instance, or even shower!

This is one reason why I don't particularly like the phrase "me-time." I feel like it conveys to the user the idea of stealing time away from others for me, and it has a seriously self-centered vibe. Instead, I view incorporating healthy tasks into my life as selfless, done in order to become stronger and healthier, and hopefully live longer for my husband, my kids, and my God.

Thursday's Action Points:

- Have you succumbed to the idea that taking time for healthy activities is selfish? Take a few minutes to write out five reasons why it is actually a way to show love to your family.
- You may not want to incorporate all of these healthy habits in your life, and I certainly don't want you to try to do all of them all at once. So pick one new healthy habit, whether it is one of these or a different one. Think of a way to make it stick. Write it down somewhere so you won't forget. Start it today or tomorrow.
- Do you have trouble being faithful in small areas of life like this? Find an accountability partner who

Bonus Week: Organizing Your Home and Life

will check in with you each day to make sure you remembered to do your new habit. It would be best if they want to incorporate this same habit in their life, or a different one of a similar nature.

Friday

USE "ROCKS, SCISSORS, PAPER" FOR PRODUCTIVITY

I have quite a few days in my life where I feel overwhelmed by the events that are planned. For instance, while I am writing this part of the book, I am hosting an eight-person mission team and overseeing most of their meals. We also are housing three extra people in our home. It's a two-week team and when they leave, we have about 48 hours before we also leave the country for a two-month overseas trip.

During the two weeks they are here, I am also trying desperately to finish our homeschool year, wrap up grades for everyone, including the extra children I teach, attend all of my children's end of the year events at our Bible college, and help my husband with all of the extra work he has going on.

Every morning I wake up feeling like it will be God's grace alone that sees me through to the end of the day.

But although I rely on that grace, I can't just sit on my hands and expect work to get done. I have to plan diligently and work hard. And I have found a three-step tool that helps me. It's called "Rocks-Scissors-Paper." But it isn't the game kids play with their hands to determine who goes first in a ball game. This is a short-cut for planning your day.

Let me explain.

Rocks

There's an illustration I have used many times in teaching on time management, although it doesn't originate with me. Here's the idea.

If you were to take a big bucket and fill it up with fist sized rocks until you couldn't put any more rocks in without them tumbling out, you would have a full bucket, right?

Not really. You could actually pour pebbles in around the rocks, then sand, then water...

And *then* the bucket would finally be full.

This illustration, which has been used many times, makes the point that if you started with the water or the sand, you would never be able to fit the rocks in. You have to start with the big rocks and then work the rest of the items in around them.

You probably plan your budget like this. You start with your rent or mortgage, then your electricity and water bills, and then you fit everything else in around those items. The most important things need to fit in first.

The same thing is true with our time. We must fill our schedule first with the rocks. They are the important things that we know we need to get done. They may include things like homeschooling or exercise. If you work, that is a rock you must fit in early before your time runs out. Sand and water that can trickle in at the end are things like TV watching, internet surfing, or other hobbies.

I know my own rocks. Even on days like today, I make a valiant effort to start my day with my own personal rocks: time reading my Bible, exercising, and providing for the needs of my family and the mission team. When I sat down to write this, it was almost 2:30. I had worked all morning (with help) to prepare and clean up the noon meal for everyone. Writing is a pebble; it's not a rock.

I start with rocks.

Scissors

And then I move to the scissors. Scissors cut, and the next most important thing to do on a busy day is to cut out all the non-essentials. I like to call this my to-don't list. On especially busy days, I take some time early in the morning to quickly make a list of non-essential items that I should *not* work on today. Some things are always on that list. Other things are only on that list some days, when my priorities require me to focus elsewhere.

Paper

Once I'm done with the scissors part of planning, I move on to paper. I have found it a huge help to write down my to-do list and my goals and appointments for the day. Some days this is 2 or 3 items. Other days it might be 20.

I try to get everything off my brain and onto paper. David Allen, author of the Getting Things Done system, calls this *capturing* and claims that it frees your brain to focus because you aren't worried about forgetting anything.

Bonus Week: Organizing Your Home and Life

When you try to live with no capturing system, your brain will be working overtime all day trying to remember everything on your mental list.

It might be easier for you to use your phone for this, or your calendar. I do have a day planner I use regularly. But for this daily stuff that will hopefully be completely done by the end of the day, I just write it down on scrap paper and throw it away when it's finished. It's a wonderful thing to go to bed at the end of the day having accomplished everything on your to-do list. I know this because once, in 2003, I did this.

Just kidding! I actually have done this many times. But it is a valid discussion point, because what about those items that get put on the paper and then never get done?

I'm glad you asked.

It depends on the item. Sometimes I throw the task away with the paper, because by the end of the day I have discovered the task no longer needs to be done. Other times I move it to the next day or the next week.

If after three or four weeks of failing to accomplish a certain task, however, I do question whether it is really something I should be doing. At that point, I either do it or I ditch it. You have to make that choice. Sometimes we procrastinate doing something because it doesn't really fit our lifestyle or our real goals. If that is the case, we can cross it off and forget about it.

Rocks-Scissors-Paper. Put the big rocks into your day and finish them first, then cut out all the non-essentials, and then write down everything else you need to get done. At the end of the day, if you focus, you will be amazed how much you have accomplished with this system!

Friday's Action Points:

- What are your big rocks, the things you should accomplish first in your day?
- What should be on your permanent to-don't list? What should you cut from your life most days?
- What paper will you use tomorrow to capture all the important tasks for the day?

Saturday

CREATE A STRONG MENTAL MODEL

"Mom, I cleaned up the living room!" My nine-year old's voice floated in to me from the other room. I smiled and went to check, knowing what I would see. The decorative pillows were centered neatly on the couch, the piano was cleaned off and closed, and each piece of furniture was exactly where it belonged. No toys were scattered on the floor. No books stacked on the coffee table. Everything was exactly where it should be.

But if I had asked any other child to do this task, it would have been a different story. The living room would be "clean" in a different way: pillows tossed haphazardly on the couch, furniture slightly askew, toys and books piled on end tables and in corners, piano open with music strewn across the top.

My nine year old has a strong mental model of what a clean living room looks like. My other children? Well, I'm still working on that.

Do you have a strong mental model of what you want your home to look like?

It doesn't need to look like mine.

Bonus Week: Organizing Your Home and Life

If I ask my other children to clean up, I know that things will be tidied up in their particular way, not mine. As hard as I have tried to communicate, they don't share my mental model.

I have a dear friend whose mental model of a living room includes a train track stretched across the floor. That's totally awesome. Her kids love it.

I have another friend whose mental model includes a piano stacked high with music. That works for her.

Your mental model does not need to look like mine, but you should have one. Sometimes the only difference between a mom whose home is tidy and one whose isn't is the mental model they have of what a home should look like.

I don't think you should strive for a home that looks like a magazine spread. A couple of times a day I make sure my home matches my mental model. Certain areas of my home have to match my mental model every single day. Other areas line up a few times a week. But here's the point: I have a very strong mental model of what it should look like at those times.

Those who have a strong mental model strive harder to match it because otherwise they experience cognitive dissonance. I am one of those people.

Some women excel at this, and by 8:00 every morning their entire house is clean and tidy and delicious smells are wafting through the house from the direction of the kitchen. Other women spend their entire day looking around them wondering where all the stuff came from and

Bonus Week: Organizing Your Home and Life

where it should go. And then they step over the piles because they really don't know what to do with them.

I have some very close friends who never experience cognitive dissonance. This can be a very good thing for them, if they don't mind living with the chaos. But I'm going to guess that if you picked this book up to read it, you mind. You want an organized homeschool and probably an organized home also. Or maybe your husband bought it for you because although you don't mind the comfy chaos that permeates your home, his perfectionistic soul craves order.

I wanted to end this chapter with this thought, not because it is the least important thought in the book, but because it is perhaps the most important thing I can possibly share.

If you really struggle with having an organized home or an organized homeschool, there is hope! You can be one of those people with a tidy home. I'm not promising you constant perfection. That would be foolish. I don't believe we should strive for that. That could make our home a very uncomfortable place for our families. Instead, I think we as moms should have a strong mental picture of what each room in our home should look like—and when—and then relax about everything else.

If your mental model of your front porch includes a skateboard and a bike, you will look at that porch, see the skateboard and bike and instead of cringing at the sight, you will sigh happily because you have healthy, active children and you are able to provide healthy, active riding toys for them. It will bring you joy.

If your mental model for your kitchen at night includes totally empty countertops and a vase of flowers, you will experience joy when you see it. But you may also have an afternoon mental model of a kitchen that looks like a hard-working bakery: flour and a rolling pin on the counter, a hand mixer tilted over a bowl of drool-worthy frosting, and the smell of yummy cupcakes in the oven. You will look at that kitchen and see not a mess, but a happy family soon clustered around the dinner table eagerly anticipating dessert.

Maybe your mental model for your bedroom in the morning includes a freshly-made bed and wide open windows letting in both sunshine and fresh air. But it could also include a messy bed because your dear husband works nightshift and comes home in the early hours to crash. If that's the case, you can be content because that is the way your bedroom is *supposed* to look like at that time.

In other words, for you to be content and joy-filled, you need to make sure that your mental model is based on reality, love, and intentionality. Don't be a perfectionist. Don't be so consumed with order and organization that your children can't have any fun! Don't be so obsessed with your Pinterest-perfect homeschool that you can't relax and enjoy leaving a book (or five) open on the coffee table.

And don't be so discouraged that your mental model includes dishes piled all over the counters twenty-four hours a day, beds that never get made, or toys that are never picked up.

Instead, sit down and talk to yourself. Instead of listening to your discontent mind spew nonsense at you, talk yourself through the way your home should be. Ask yourself what your expectation is for each room. How often should it look that way? Who should be in charge of getting it to that level of tidiness? What will fill your rooms with laughter and your home with love and fun? What level of tidiness does your family need to have in order to operate on a reasonable level of peace and productivity?

Don't adopt other people's mental models. Be proactive and create your own.

And don't hesitate to change those as needed. Your life will change. Your husband will get a first shift job. Your baby will stop nursing through the night. Your teenagers will graduate and leave the house. With new mental models in place, you can maintain continuity for your family even when things like this rock your world.

You are in charge.

You've got this.

Now go and make a difference in your home.

Saturday's Action Points:

- Sit down with a cup of coffee or tea and take a few minutes to write down your mental model for what each area of your home should look like.
- How often should it look like that? When?
- How can you get it to look like that?

- Who should be in charge of these areas? Do you need to delegate some chores to some children?
- Who are you most tempted to emulate? Is that a good thing or a bad thing? In what way is their lifestyle different from yours?
- Do you tend to be too perfectionistic or too lax? What can you do to be more balanced? Is there someone you trust who can hold you accountable for this?

Chapter 7

HOMESCHOOLING IN CHALLENGING PLACES

In an ideal world, we would never have to homeschool in challenging times or in challenging places. However, sometimes it happens, doesn't it? We end up homeschooling in other people's houses, in our car, or in doctor's offices.

Life is rarely ideal.

In this chapter, I'd like to address two challenging places to homeschool: your master bedroom and your car.

Homeschooling in your master bedroom

Earlier in this book I said that if you have any other places to homeschool, don't do it in your master bedroom.

I mean every word I write. But this year, in my current situation, that is the only place I have left in the house to homeschool my kindergarten-age twins.

So I'm learning to make the best of my situation.

It is not ideal. It is not what I would have wished. But I am certain that there are other families out there who, because of whatever circumstances may be in their lives right now, are forced to homeschool in their master bedrooms. And if you are one of those people, let me encourage you to do it with joy and flair! Make the best of your circumstances.

There are two verses in the Bible that have meant a lot to me in my situation this year:

- "I can do all things through Christ which strengtheneth me" (Philippians 4:13).
- "Do all things without murmurings or disputings" (Philippians 2:14).

See, the thing is, homeschooling two kindergarteners in my bedroom is not the end of it all. This choice has consequences.

Because I'm stuck in there with them to oversee their education (which feels like it consists mostly of crayons, scissors, and glue), I also end up doing all the grading and checking of my other kids' work in there also. That means Teacher's manuals. Files. Our family Homeschool Binder. Lots of extra papers and equipment. All of this extra stuff, in turn, means an extra bookshelf.

My bedroom—my lovely, peaceful haven of rest and nourisher of my marriage—has been overrun with homeschool stuff.

I can't live like that, so I have come up with some guidelines for myself. These may also be helpful to you, if you are in a similar situation.

Organize and stay that way.

Begin by decluttering your master bedroom of all extraneous items. If it doesn't relate to things that need to take place in your bedroom, try to find another place for it. (Or give it away to someone in need!)

Once you have decluttered, containerize everything you possibly can. Look for pieces of furniture or baskets or other container possibilities for all of the many things that are part and parcel with homeschooling. Hide and camouflage as much as possible. Out of sight, out of mind will help you flip the mental switch from homeschool mom to romantic wife.

Keep everything attractive and in line with the style of your room.

One large piece of furniture is less visually distracting than many smaller pieces. Is there a piece of furniture, such as a sideboard with drawers or a wardrobe that you could use that would be able to hold most or all of your homeschool items? These often have drawers in them, perfect for holding all of the little manipulatives as well as larger items like a three-hole punch. Or can you convert a closet into a homeschool center? Or use a bookshelf with baskets for smaller items?

As much as possible, use neutral colors or color-coordinate your binders and storage containers with your bedding and curtains.

Keep school within working hours.

I have found that limiting my time actually makes me more productive. It exerts a positive effect on my schedule. Can you plan a cut-off time for your school day and try to religiously stick to it? Your work may not be done at the end of that time, but you can still be done with your work!

Don't sacrifice your sleep on the altar of homeschooling. Sleep is vitally important for all of us, but especially if we hope to be kind and patient with our children the next day. Make sure you keep your homeschooling within working hours so that you, your husband, and your children can all get the rest you need.

Become a minimalist.

I try very hard to minimize distractions for my kindergarteners. I have a "no stuff" rule that we try to uphold most of the time. My boys know that they are not to bring toys, stuffed animals, blankets, pillows, umbrellas, rocks, insects, or dead animals into my bedroom. Books are allowed but they must go back out at the end of the school day if they don't belong in our current "reading basket."

School stuff, in and of itself, can take over your life. Try to put a cap on it! And definitely do your best to encourage your children to keep their personal items where they belong.

Tidy up every day.

Our K-5 curriculum is awesome. But it involves so much cutting, gluing and coloring that at the end of the school day my bedroom floor always looks like a ticker-tape parade just marched through. I have hardwood floors, so I bought a broom and dustpan that is specifically for sweeping upstairs just so I wouldn't have to go searching for my broom every day. My twins sweep up after themselves every day at the end of their schoolwork. And I myself am cultivating the discipline of putting everything away in the afternoon so my husband and I can enjoy our bedroom at night.

Don't let homeschooling affect your romance.

Your bedroom is primarily for rest and romance. Only secondarily is it for school. Keep your priorities straight, and definitely do your best to keep your homeschool stress out of your love life! Your husband will appreciate it.

Homeschooling in your bedroom may not be ideal, but it is workable! It just requires a little more organization at the end of your school hours in order to tidy up. But there is one more place you may have to homeschool that is far more challenging.

Homeschooling in your car

If you do a lot of travelling together as a family, you will have the unique task of homeschooling in the car (or boat, train, or plane). This adds a whole new dynamic. Yet, there are ways to take the principles of this book and repurpose them for a car.

For instance, you still need equipment. You still need to have all supplies within arm's reach (this is actually more of a necessity in a car). You need an even firmer grasp of your curriculum and what you must accomplish each week, because you need to take all the supplies necessary for the work to be completed. You must keep rigid records of everything, especially since it is easy to lose or misplace papers while transferring from one place to another.

All of these challenges are opportunities for success or failure. But each one is surmountable.

Here are some ideas from my own experience as well as that of friends.

Your "home base" can be the place where you set up your curriculum, just like you would in your homeschool room. If necessary, it can be as simple as a row of books on the floor with suitcases as bookends.

When you make a pit stop at your home base, you will need to gather all the materials you need for your next extended trip. It would be impossible for my family, for instance, to take all of our curriculum with us on our travels. There would be no room for clothes! Here are some tips for isolating and taking the most important parts of the curriculum:

Teachers Manuals

If your teacher's manuals come with spiral binding, untwist the wire and remove it. Immediately replace it with lockable rings. These come in all sizes, so you will be able to find some that are just the right size for every book. Now, when you travel, after you make your weekly sheets of lessons to accomplish, collect those portions from each teacher's manual to take with you. Snap them into a new set of rings, ones in which you will keep all your teacher's manuals from every subject for every child. If you have a lot of different classes/children that you are doing this for, you will want to use dividers for this makeshift binder, or even make yourself sturdy covers of some sort. Slip this into some kind of carrier: Either a manila envelope or a plastic case of some sort.

Be choosy about what you take. Can you teach the lesson without the teacher's manual? For many of the younger grades, you certainly could! If your children are using DVDs, how much of the manual do you actually need? Some DVDs, for instance, come with several sets of "guides" that provide the answer keys to all the necessary pages. Those pages are three-hole punched and are ideal for slipping out of one binder and into another. For a primary-aged child, you may not even need that! You can add the two digit numbers for their math worksheets without an answer key. Take only what you need.

Alternatives:

- Use a file folder or pocket for your teacher's edition pages.
- For the tech-savvy: Use your tablet or cell phone to photograph the pages you will need. File them carefully for easy access.

Worktext Pages

For your children's pages, give them each a three-ring binder. Ideally, it would zipper closed and have dividers inside for each subject. Three-hole punch all the pages that they will need for the lessons they are to accomplish on

Homeschooling in Challenging Places

that trip and insert them into their notebook. Try to include any other extras, but realize that you can always substitute. For instance, if they need counting cubes for Math, you could always use pennies or some other kind of counters. For paper counters or other small manipulatives, slide them into a large envelop or sealable pouch you can insert into their binder. Keep a couple of pencils in their zippered notebook or in a pouch in the notebook. Include everything: tests, lesson pages, etc. If your trip isn't too long, you will not need to take the Test Answer Keys with you. Simply file their tests and take them home for grading.

Textbooks

For textbooks, you have three options: pack them all, perform surgery on the textbook to remove the necessary pages, or purchase electronic textbooks. These are becoming more prevalent and, with the advent of electronic readers and free ebook apps for tablets and laptops, easily acquired.

School Supplies

Create a homeschool supply box. Use a shoebox or a toolbox that can easily fit in your car or under a seat in your van. Many of these have a slide-out top with a handle for easy access to smaller items. Pick one that can hold pencils, pens, crayons, scissors, glue, tape, a ruler, and a small stapler. All of these are necessary homeschool items. This can be the one-stop shop for supplies, and everyone can borrow from it as necessary.

If you have little children who like to be a part of what is going on around them, pack a crayon book or two for them to do "school" with. It will minimize problems while you are distracted with the older children.

Record Keeping on the Road

Record keeping is challenging enough for homeschool moms at home. Keeping track of homework, test, and quiz grades on the road can be a hassle! It is easy to lose papers, and you need to keep grades in a trustworthy place.

For mobile records that are travel friendly, use your laptop, cellphone, or tablet to keep track of grades. You can take this with you wherever you go. For security purposes, back up your files.

If you grade on the road, you can throw all the papers away except for the ones that will be needed for reporting to your state at the end of the year. This is a big blessing. Some families will find it easier just to keep everything and grade when they return home. On the other hand, you could also take a picture of any pages you need to keep. This could be printed in case you lose the actual paper.

Never forget that travel is an education in and of itself! Your children are learning by doing, not just by reading, when you travel. Take pictures of them at the Grand Canyon, the Liberty Bell, and other monuments, museums, or historical sites for both their scrapbook and their homeschool records. Have them write a short paper or report about what they learned. Glue the picture to the report and slide it into a page protector for safety. Give them credit for field trips.

You can take your travels a step further and help your

children start a blog to share their adventures with family and friends. Let them type their reports about the places they visit, or (if they are young) type for them as they dictate to you. (You will be surprised by how fascinating their reports become when they can dictate them to someone else and don't have to worry about spelling all those challenging words!) Teach them to crop and edit pictures using an online editing tool.

If you are road-tripping with your homeschooling family, you will face unique challenges in keeping your curriculum in order, providing suitable study times, and keeping efficient records. View these as an opportunity for creativity instead of a burden, and you will be amazed at the solutions God will bring to your mind.

Chapter 8

CONQUERING HOMESCHOOL CLUTTER

Have you ever tried to focus on teaching math while your toddler stood by your chair pulling on your shirt and chanting, "Mommy, can I have a snack? Mommy, can I go outside to play? Mommy, can you read to me? Mommy, can you play a game with me? Mommy, can I eat cereal?"

It's impossible, isn't it? You are more likely to get frustrated and annoyed with your toddler than to successfully teach Algebra to your middle schooler.

The same thing, however, is also true when it is not your toddler, but your environment screaming at you.

Scientists from the Princeton University Neuroscience Institute did a study on clutter in the visual field and came to this conclusion, paraphrased by Erin Doland[1]: "When your environment is cluttered, the chaos restricts your ability to focus. The clutter also limits your brain's ability to process information. Clutter makes you distracted and unable to process information as well as you do in an uncluttered, organized, and serene environment."

In other words, when your schoolroom or your home is cluttered and full of visual disorder, your brain (and your child's brain) will have a hard time focusing on their schoolwork and instead will feel frustrated by their studies.

My desk tends to get cluttered very easily. My children bring me tests to grade and they end up on my desk. My husband writes something that he wants me to edit and it ends up on my desk. I have my devotions and my journal sits there on my desk. All of these things rob me of focus when I sit down to write, teach, or do some grading.

Take a look around the area where your child studies. What is robbing them of their focus?

If you completed the three-week challenge in this book, you already took control of that clutter and disorganization and created a healthy environment for focus and study. But once you have decluttered and organized your schoolroom or home, how can you keep it that way?

---

[1] https://unclutterer.com/2011/03/29/scientists-find-physical-clutter-negatively-affects-your-ability-to-focus-process-information/

Conquering Homeschool Clutter

Things you can do to Declutter

When trying to declutter, start by analyzing the problem areas that tend to mushroom or spread clutter. For some families, like mine, it may be mom's desk. For others, it is the kitchen counter. Maybe it is your coffee table, where mail piles up, or the foyer just inside your door. Pinpoint the top one or two problem areas in your home and then hound them. Don't allow clutter to begin to fester. Arrange a pretty vase of flowers or something else there that will remind everyone not to just plop things down whenever and wherever but to put things in their place.

Secondly, institute a quick 10-minute cleanup at the end of your homeschool day. Everyone should participate. So this doesn't spill over too much into your kids' free time, set a kitchen timer and then sic them on the clutter. A small snack afterwards could be a reward for their efforts.

While decluttering, make it a point to focus on the area where your child studies. Do you have a schoolroom? Strip out anything that is not school related. Do your children study at the dining room table? Fold your laundry somewhere else. Do they study at a desk in their bedroom? Bedroom cleanup every morning should be mandatory.

In the midst of decluttering your home and homeschool stuff, take time to address your own personal clutter issues. Set a good example! If you want your child to make their bed, make yours. If you want your child to clean off their desk, clean off yours!

Lastly, always take care of the biggest problems first. Beds get made every morning in our house, because I believe bed-making is a keystone habit, the kind of habit that sparks off other helpful habits. It is also the biggest item in a bedroom, so when the bed is made the room instantly looks tidier.

What is your biggest problem area? Attack it today and help your child focus better on his schoolwork.

It isn't just our normal home items that degenerate into piles of clutter, though. Homeschooling clutter is a major factor for most homeschooling moms. What are some of these things?

Homeschool Clutter

Curriculum. Planners. Log books. Portfolios. Curriculum catalogues. Math manipulatives. Flashcards. The list of possible homeschool clutter can go on forever. If you don't mind your homeschool stuff taking over your house, your time, and your life, collect it all and have some great homeschool fun.

But me? I mind.

I want a life in addition to homeschooling. (This is a choice I have made; your choice may be different and that's okay.)

I'm on a quest to minimize the homeschool stuff I own and, more particularly, the stuff that is out and about in my house. (I don't mind storing items that I will use in the future and that will save me money. I just object to these things getting mixed into toys and being scattered all over.)

Conquering Homeschool Clutter

What are some of the things that tend to clutter up our homeschools?

Portfolios

You need them in order to satisfy state laws. But can you assemble them at the end of the year? I store all my kids' keepable stuff in one large 2 inch binder. At this point I don't need to assemble individual portfolios, but if I do need to, I will do it later, when the need arises.

You may find it more helpful, though, to go ahead and begin assembling a portfolio for each child at the beginning of the school year. That's fine. But have you put last year's portfolios into storage? Especially if you are the mom of a large family, you will want to ruthlessly narrow down the number of portfolios taking up prime real estate in your homeschool. (Do the math: if you homeschool six children for 12 years each, that's 72 portfolios.)

Unused Curriculum

Over the years I have learned that my family does best with a "Curriculum in a Box" style. I use BJU Press, in a combination of video and non-video classes. It pushes all my buttons. As comprehensive and plentiful of a curriculum it is, it nonetheless saves me from collecting outside curricula. I have tried—and failed—to interest myself and my children in other awesome types of curricula, so now I try to focus on keeping those books that come with that one curriculum. This helps me to reign in any impulse to multiply unto myself other homeschool books that would ultimately become clutter.

Kindergarten Crafts

If you have a robust Kindergarten curriculum like I do, you have multiple new projects going on daily. We make scepters and crowns, police hats and badges, dioramas, and a thousand other paper-based projects each quarter. If I saved them all, our furniture would have to go on the back porch. And I don't have a back porch.

So I save them for about a week. If they are really special, maybe for a month. Sometimes I have to wait until my boys forget about them. Then I take a picture and throw them out ruthlessly. If you need to do it more quickly than that, display them for a few days, hide them for a few days, and then throw them out. My kids are pack rats and would keep every single one forever-and-ever-amen if I let them.

Homeschool Curriculum Catalogs

I don't collect them and I don't keep them. Why look at something designed to make me want more than I need? That's my version of serving myself a heaping tablespoon of discontentment.

Here's the thing: you and I have a limited amount of hard drive space that can be devoted to making decisions each day. As homeschooling moms, we face enormous amounts of curriculum options. If you love experimenting, these may not be clutter to you. But I have to save my decision-making ability for the really important things in my life, like what's for dinner. I can't use it all up on yearly curriculum decisions. If I already know what curriculum I plan to use, all the other catalogs are merely clutter. That's my story, and I'm sticking to it.

Older Editions of Textbooks

Are you still able to use it? Great. If not, it needs to go.

Faulty School Supplies

If a pen doesn't work, or if it skips or bleeds ink, throw it away. While you are at it, throw away all those pencils with lead that is too light to read. Invest in some with #2 lead. Check your highlighters and markers also.

Broken rulers? Staplers that constantly stick? Hole punchers that don't punch? Glue so hard you could use it as a hammer? Tape that won't unroll? Rusty paperclips? Get rid of them all.

Art Supplies

Have a storage solution for all of your art supplies and don't go beyond it. If your supplies exceed your storage space, start throwing away or donating.

Homeschool families collect clutter like your husband's best suit collects cat hair. Over time, all that clutter begins to overwhelm us and steal our focus. We must conquer our clutter in order to be able study and work without distraction. But what can you do with homeschool clutter?

How to Conquer Clutter

You cannot organize clutter. Clutter multiplies, stealing your time, attention, and money. Have you ever decided to stay home from a family outing because your house was so cluttered that you felt like it was more important to declutter and organize than to be with your family? That is clutter stealing time from your family! Have you ever invested in a storage unit because you couldn't get rid of things? That is clutter stealing your money. Do you have a hard time focusing on homeschooling or housework because you have too much stuff staring you in your face? That is clutter stealing your attention.

You must conquer your clutter by getting rid of it. Today. Before it steals more time, money, and attention from the things and people that really matter to you.

How can you do this?

First, cull courageously.

If you haven't used it in the last five years (or for the last five kids), how can you possibly think you might use it for the next five (years or kids)? Be courageous as you clutter. Ask yourself this question, "What is the worst thing that can possibly happen if I get rid of this?" Usually it isn't very big, especially for the items that are truly clutter.

If you can't stomach a full-scale declutter attack, start small. Tell yourself you will find one item every day that you will get rid of. Don't go to bed until you have committed that one item to your "get rid of" pile.

But I know: you hate to get rid of items that still have a monetary value, right? So sell them at yard sales, curriculum fairs, or online stores. For a little bit of work setting up a table and pricing your unused clutter, you could make some money.

However, if time is of the essence for you, take the dare to donate.

For charity, donate to thrift stores. Or offer your items for free to various homeschool groups, churches, or friends.

Conquering Homeschool Clutter

If you have a heart to truly make the world a better place, try donating to schools and mothers in third world countries. You get bonus points for figuring out a way to donate compassionately like this. I have travelled through many third-world countries where there are mothers just like you and me, with a heart for educating their children, who struggle to find the funds to buy simple textbooks and other education supplies.

Yes, in many of those places English textbooks aren't usable. But there are places where they are. If you know any people in other countries, contact them and ask if there is a way you can donate for the needs of the country. Homeschooling moms aren't the only ones who could use books; schools also need educational supplies. Look specifically for countries where English is used in their educational system.

You can make a difference in someone's world by donating the things you don't need.

Thirdly, keep a memento, not the actual item.

Use your cell phone! Snap a photo of the artwork, take a video of the volcano as it explodes, or archive a soft copy of all of the journal pages or papers your child writes. Then throw away the artwork, volcano, and whatever else is not deemed keep-worthy. Get input from your children. Ask yourself if this is really something your child wants to take into marriage with them. If not, do them and you a favor and get rid of it now. Keep a memento to prove to them, yourself, and your state government officials that they actually did it, made it, experimented with it, or wrote it.

Conquering Homeschool Clutter

If your kids insist on keeping absolutely everything—and some children do—grant them a specific amount of time to enjoy it. Then take your picture, hold a funeral, and move on with life. Encourage them to choose only the best of the best for keeping permanently.

Homeschooling doesn't have to turn our whole house into disarray. Students of all ages learn better in a tidy, organized environment. Take steps today to make your homeschool clutter-free!

WHAT'S NEXT?

Thank you for reading this book. I truly hope it was a blessing to you.

First, I'd like to remind you that all of the printables mentioned in this book are available for download from HomeschoolWithAMission.weebly.com. In addition, I have made a printable checklist for you that includes all of the daily action steps outlined in this book. For quick reference, print that out before you begin your three week transformation.

Secondly, I would like to invite you to read the companion book to this one, *Life Management for the Busy Homeschooling Mother*. It will give you eight intensely practical strategies for creating a peaceful home and life.

And finally, I'd also like to ask you for a favor. Although it will only take a few seconds of your time, it would be a big help to me.

To authors, reviews are a blessing. Honest reviews can direct readers to good books and help an author to know how to improve their writing or content. Would you take a minute to leave a honest review for this book on the website where you purchased it?

Thank you!

Laura Berrey

WORKSHEETS AND CHECKLISTS

WEEK ONE CHECKLIST
Organizing Your Schoolroom

Monday: Choose your schoolroom location.

- Walk through your house (mentally or physically), and consider each room. Think through the pros and cons of using each space. Decide where you will homeschool this year.
- If you choose to homeschool in multiple locations, is there one place where you can keep all the supplies and books corralled? Things could be taken from there and returned again in order to maintain tidiness throughout the rest of the house.

Tuesday: Plan your schoolroom for maximum efficiency.

- Consider your curriculum and make a list of everything you will need for your schoolroom. Ideally, schoolbooks and supplies will be close to the study area.
- Small children need shorter-sized furniture. Consider old school desks or student chairs. Can you cut down an old table? Can you use a coffee table?
- Do you have the furniture you need? Measure your space. Measure your furniture. Will it fit? If not, what can you substitute? If your room has a closet

in it, consider building shelves for school books directly into the closet.
- Once you have foraged in your house for furniture to repurpose, if you still have needs, make a shopping list. Check out Craig's list and other internet sites before Thursday.
- Don't forget what kind of necessities you need: desk, table, chairs, book shelves, bulletin board, whiteboard, trash can, and a photocopier or printer.
- Spend any extra time you have today moving furniture and any other items out of your homeschool room in preparation for cleaning it.

Wednesday: Thoroughly clean your schoolroom or school area.

- Gather your cleaning supplies and, if possible, a troop of helpers. Move everything out of the room. (Don't forget to empty the closet.) Collect a batch of boxes and store anything left in the room. Organize the boxes with like items. Label every box! Store in an out-of-the-way location.
- Take down the curtains and wash them.
- Unscrew any light fixtures and put them in the sink to soak.
- Start with the ceiling and work your way down the walls to the floor. Clean it completely. Try to do it as quickly as possible.
- Put away your cleaning supplies, screw light fixtures back on, and replace your curtains or purchase new ones.

Thursday: Shop for schoolroom furniture and supplies.

- Fix your budget. Stay within it.
- Be creative in where you look. If you don't find everything you need today, make do while you keep on looking.
- Be creative in where you shop.
- Take your diagram (or measurements) of the room, just in case you have questions while looking at a piece of furniture.
- Follow your color scheme.

Friday: Assemble your schoolroom.

- Set up your room schoolroom for maximum efficiency.
- Think through your storage and shelving options.
- Keep school items within easy reach.
- Try to keep all toys out of the room.
- If you have younger children who are not schooling, plan your schedule and room in a way that enables them to be included or not, as needed.

Saturday: Help your children to "own" their study space.

- Give each child their own space.
- Help them to decorate it.
- Provide all the necessary school supplies in a logical location.
- Make a list of any supplies you still need.

WEEK TWO CHECKLIST
Organizing Your Curriculum

Monday: Gather all your curriculum into one location.

- Collect all the pieces for your curriculum this year. Don't forget the things you have in storage!
- Treasure hunt for school and office supplies for your school room.
- Start a list of things you know you need to purchase.

Tuesday: Organize your curriculum.

- Arrange each child's student materials on a shelf or in a crate.
- Arrange all of your teacher materials in one location, organized first by child and then by subject.
- Separate all tests and test answer keys.

Wednesday: Shop or forage for supplies.

- Armed with your lists, go shopping.
- While you are running your errands, scout out other organizational tools that could make your life easier.
- Don't give up on something if you don't find it in the expected department. If you are looking in the office or school supply department and don't find what you need, check the hardware department or

the bathroom department. Be creative!

- If you have several children, color code their supplies as much as possible. This makes your life—and theirs—so much more efficient and orderly.

Thursday: Organize your extras.

- Store all the extras related to your curriculum in the closet or nearby storage area.
- Have your children help with organizing school supplies.
- Each child should have certain school supplies at their own desk: crayons, pencils, pens, etc. Keep extras in a central location such as a tool box or hanging shoe holder with transparent pockets.
- Each child should have a three-ring binder and a small clipboard, preferably in their own designated color.
- Think through your clutter headaches. Isolate the problem, brainstorm ideas, give your solutions a try, and when all else fails, box it up!

Friday: Set up your file box.

- Set up your file box. File your tests, test answer keys, and any other papers you need on hand for this school year.
- Anything related to classes not being taught this year should be stacked with all the rest of your curriculum outside of the schoolroom area.

Saturday: Establish your long-term curriculum storage.

- Designate a location for unused homeschool materials. Box them up by grade levels and store them in a protected place.
- Store all of your files for the past school year in a filing cabinet or a file box.

WEEK THREE CHECKLIST
Organizing Your Record Keeping

Monday: Assemble your family homeschool notebook.

- Download your free Family Homeschool Binder. Assemble it.
- Assemble your children's three-ring binders.

Tuesday: Make your goals for the year.

- Using the Goals Sheet, fill out goals for each of the subject areas your child will study.
- Fill out goals for each of the skill sets you want your child to conquer.
- Ask your child about their interests and what they want to learn this year. It might surprise you.
- Get feedback from both your husband and your children about extra-curricular goals for each subject area and skill set.

Wednesday: Prepare your school year calendar.

- Using the Calendar sheet, mark your beginning and end dates.
- Mark off any dates you know you cannot have school. Plan the weeks and days you will do school.
- Schedule vacations, field trips, and other fun events.

Thursday: Make a daily schedule.

- Fill out your daily schedule. Don't forget to

schedule times of teaching as well as overseeing piano practice, cooking dinner, grocery shopping, running errands, and any other weekly duties.
- Fill out a schedule for each child. This could be a block format or an hour-by-hour format.
- Live by your schedule but maintain flexibility within your routine.

Friday: Overview your curriculum.

- Take a good look at each subject. Order any special equipment or materials you need for that course.
- Find out how many lessons/pages there are in the course. From that information, plan out how much you need to finish in one week. Write that on your goals sheet.

Saturday: Compile your lesson plans.

- Fill out the first week's lesson plan for each course each child will take. Keep these in your Family Homeschool Notebook so that you won't lose them.
- Give your child an assignment sheet to check off. Clip it to their clipboard and show them how to use it. Either write the lessons they should do on their assignment sheet or, if they already know to do one lesson or page a day, have them write down the lessons they accomplished.
- Clip their assignment sheet to their clipboard and prop it up on their study area so that they are ready to start their first week of the homeschool year!

WEEK FOUR CHECKLIST
Organizing Your Life and Home

Monday: Figure out your "Five Under Five" tasks.

- List the 5 most important tasks you can do to keep your home running smoothly, and how you can accomplish them early in your day.
- Time yourself, and try to beat the five minute deadline for each. Afterwards, ask yourself what you could have done to streamline the process. Could you do all five tasks in 15 minutes? Ten? What would it take?
- Whatever your tasks are, and however many you have, write them down right now on a three by five card. Keep it in a visible place until you have done them so many times you can accomplish them in your sleep.
- Number your tasks in the logical order in which you should do them.
- Ask a friend or family member to hold you accountable for the first ten days of doing this list. If you can do them every day for ten days, you will be well on your way to creating a habit!

Tuesday: Simplify with meal planning.

- Pick a simple method of meal planning and make a list of meals for the rest of this week.
- Make a list for next week.

- Want to make your year easier? Make a four-week list and rotate it every month.
- Take it a step further and create one four-week list for each season of the year.

Wednesday: Launch your campaign against dirty laundry.
- Fill in the blanks for the laundry worksheet.
- Inform your family of any changes.
- Teach your children to properly put away their laundry in their drawers and closets.
- Train your family in daily putting dirty laundry where it belongs.
- Purchase any needed equipment or supplies.

Thursday: Maintain healthy habits.
- Have you succumbed to the idea that taking time for healthy activities is selfish? Take a few minutes to write out five reasons why it is actually a way to show love to your family.
- Pick one new healthy habit. Think of a way to make it stick. Write it down somewhere so you won't forget. Start it today or tomorrow.
- Do you have trouble being faithful in small areas of life like this? Find an accountability partner who will check in with you each day to make sure you remembered to do your new habit. It would be best if they want to incorporate a similar habit in their life.

Friday: Use "Rocks, Scissors, Paper" for productivity.
- What are your big rocks, the things you should

accomplish first in your day?
- What should be on your permanent to-don't list? What should you cut from your life?
- What paper will you use tomorrow to capture all the important tasks for the day?

Saturday: Create a strong mental model.
- Describe your mental model for what each area of your home should look like.
- How often should it look like that? When?
- How can you get it to look like that?
- Who should be in charge of these areas? Do you need to delegate some chores to some children?
- Who are you most tempted to emulate? Is that a good thing or a bad thing? In what way is their lifestyle different from yours?
- Do you tend to be too perfectionistic or too lax? What can you do to be more balanced? Is there someone you trust who can hold you accountable for this?

LAUNDRY WORKSHEET
Creating a Simple System for Laundry

My dirty laundry location:

Who will collect the dirty laundry:

When will it be collected:

How often will it be collected:

How I sort laundry:

How I prepare laundry for the washing machine:

How I pretreat laundry:

When I start my first load:

Reboot Times:

How I fold my laundry:

How I hang my laundry:

When I will iron:

When I will sort and transport laundry:

Who will put it away:

ABOUT THE AUTHOR

Laura Berrey is a missionary wife and busy homeschooling mom of six children. Since 2003, she has travelled with her family to countries in Asia, Europe, and Africa so that her husband could teach, preach, and train pastors. They currently live in Metro Manila. You can connect with her at:

Livewithamission.com
and
Homeschoolwithamission.weebly.com

ALSO AVAILABLE BY LAURA BERREY

Made in United States
Orlando, FL
19 August 2023